Housing Vouchers:
An International Analysis

Housing Vouchers:
An International Analysis

E. Jay Howenstine

CENTER
FOR URBAN
POLICY RESEARCH

Published in the United States of America
by the Center for Urban Policy Research
Building 4051—Kilmer Campus
New Brunswick, New Jersey 08903

Library of Congress Cataloging-in-Publication Data

Howenstine, E. Jay (Emanuel Jay)
Housing vouchers, an international analysis.

Bibliography: p. 177
Includes index.
1.   Rent subsidies.   I.   Title.
HD7288.83.H69   1985   363.5'8   85-18323
ISBN 0-88285-111-X

CONTENTS

LIST OF TABLES

Preface

Housing vouchers provide cash assistance to low-income households to help pay the rent for a minimum-standard dwelling they cannot afford. The voucher is not tied to a particular unit; it is paid directly either to the program participant or the landlord.

The idea of a voucher—that is, a consumer housing subsidy—is not new in the United States. The Housing and Urban Development Act of 1965 established a leased-housing program under Section 23. Administered by public-housing authorities, the program involved direct payments to landlords on behalf of tenants to reduce excessive burdens. In 1972 the Department of Housing and Urban Development (HUD) launched a 10-year Experimental Housing Allowance Program (EHAP), which paid monthly housing allowances to more than 30,000 families in 12 locations. Drawing on EHAP experience, an Existing Housing Program was created in the Section 8 program of the Housing and Community Development Act of 1974. This program continues to make housing affordable for more than 800,000 households by paying a monthly stipend to the landlord on behalf of low-income tenants living in privately owned, existing housing. When other forms of Section 8 assistance are added to the Existing Housing Program, an estimated total of around 2,139,000 lower-income households will receive payments in 1985.

The President's Commission on Housing, in its final report in 1982, declared that "affordability is the primary housing problem of the poor" and recommended that:

"The primary Federal program for helping low-income families to achieve decent housing should be a Housing Payments Program. This program, coupled with housing supply assistance through the Community Development Block Grant Program, should replace future commitments to build or substantially rehabilitate additional units under Federal housing programs."[1]

In July, 1984, HUD embarked on a new housing demonstration, under the Housing and Rural Recovery Act of 1984, to compare and test certain features of the Section 8 Existing Housing Program and the voucher program. The new demonstration provides vouchers to 4,543 very-low-income families living in privately owned, existing housing in 20 cities. In launching the demonstration, Secretary of Housing Samuel R. Pierce, Jr. stated, "We believe it has the potential to shape housing policy for decades to come."[2]

Among foreign governments the idea of a consumer housing subsidy is a highly developed concept. Housing allowances, shelter allowances, rent allowances—or rent rebates as they are variously called (the term "housing voucher" is rarely used)—have been paid out on a larger scale for longer periods of time on an entitlement basis, with a much greater variety of rationales than in this country. As the United States moves ahead with its new demonstration program, it is timely to examine and evaluate foreign experiences with the consumer housing subsidy approach.

This study is divided into three major parts. The first part reviews the historical background and analyzes the various housing allowance strategies that foreign governments have adopted. The second part examines in detail the major principles and elements with which governments have fashioned their systems. The accent is on issues of maximum relevance to the American scene, and an attempt is made to define quantitatively the place of housing allowances in national housing subsidy policy. In the third part the impact of housing allowance systems is weighed in the light of the original objectives. Conclusions are also drawn about foreign experiences with respect to two central policy issues: 1) Should financial assistance to low-income families be in the form of consumer housing subsidies or producer housing subsidies, or in some synthesis of the two systems? 2) Should the housing allowance be maintained as a separate housing policy, or should it be integrated into a general income maintenance policy?

The author wishes to thank numerous persons who have provided valuable assistance to this study. They are as follows: Australia: Warwick Temby, Department of Housing and Construction, Canberra; Belgium: J. Bouillon, Secretary General, Institut National de Logement, Brussels; Canada: Frances Cameron, Director, Planning Division, and Maurice

Rabot, Manager, International Relations, Canada Mortgage and Housing Corporation, Ottawa; Professor Marion Steele, Department of Economics, University of Guelph, Guelph, Ontario; and Janet McClain, Director, Housing Programs, Canadian Council on Social Development, Ottawa; Denmark: Hanne Victor Hansen, International Relations Division, Ministry of Housing, Copenhagen; Federal Republic of Germany: Eugen Dick and Horst Bolting, Ministry for Regional Planning, Building, and Urban Development, Bonn; Finland: Keijo Tanner, National Housing Board, Helsinki; France: D. Loudenot, Civil Administrator, A. Weber, Civil Administrator, and A. Talmant, Ministry of City Planning and Housing, Paris; the Netherlands: Loek Kampschoer, Deputy Inspector General, Ministry of Housing, Physical Planning and Environment, The Hague; and Hugo Priemus, Professor of Housing, Technische Hogeschool, Delft; Norway: Egil Tombre, Director, and Tor Bysveen, Norsk Institut for By-og Regionforskning, Oslo; Sweden: Bo Loon, Research Secretary, Swedish Council for Building Research, Stockholm; Per Ahren, Housing Division, and Ian MacArthur, Administrator, International Department, Ministry of Housing and Physical Planning, Stockholm; Switzerland: K. Baumgartner, Secretary, Federal Housing Office, Bern; and A. Naef, ORL–Institute, Zurich; United Kingdom: P. R. T. Martin, Housing Al Division, Department of the Environment, London; and Michael John Oxley, Principal Lecturer in Urban Land Economics, Leicester Polytechnic, Leicester; United States: Ray Struyk, Director, Center for International Activities, Urban Institute, Washington, D.C.; J. Barry Cullingworth, College of Urban Affairs and Public Policy, University of Delaware, Newark; Martin Levine, Congressional Budget Office, Washington, D.C.; Duncan MacRae, Robert Buckley, Duane McGough, Terrence Connell, Jane Karadbil, Howard Hammerman, and Robert Gray, Office of Policy Development and Research, Department of Housing and Urban Development, Washington, D.C.

The author is the International Research Coordinator in the Office of Policy Development and Research at the U.S. Department of Housing and Urban Development, Washington, D.C. The views expressed are those of the author and do not necessarily reflect those of the Department of Housing and Urban Development.

NOTES

1. U.S., President, Commission on Housing, *The Report of the President's Commission on Housing* (Washington, D.C.: Government Printing Office, 1982), 18-19.

2. Samuel R. Pierce, Jr., *Statement at the News Conference and Briefing on HUD's Voucher Program* (Washington, D.C.: U.S. Department of Housing and Urban Development, 1984), 1.

Summary

Beginning in the 1940s the housing voucher (or housing allowance) concept inched its way into European housing policy following many different routes.

The earliest developments in the housing allowance were motivated mainly by compassion for two needy groups—the large family and the elderly—as they struggled to make ends meet. A later, more sophisticated, rationale employed the housing allowance as a means of relieving individual hardships which inevitably accompany a relaxation of wartime rent controls, so that individual households would not suffer unduly as the general social welfare was advanced through a realignment of prices in the housing market. In other cases the allowance was used in a pragmatic attempt to cope with the growing gap between the rents of new housing built at high cost levels and the rents of the existing housing stock built at much lower cost levels. Thus, people were provided with an incentive to move into new projects that might otherwise remain vacant.

Often, two conflicting motifs played important roles in the development of housing allowance systems. On the one hand, there has been a strong desire to preserve social stability by providing an allowance that strengthens the ability of financially weak households to keep the housing they have. On the other hand, an increasingly important objective has been to promote the labor mobility required by national economic growth and changing job markets. A housing allowance can be an effective tool in inducing families with grown children to move from large, low-rent, centrally located apartments to smaller, high-rent, newly constructed apartments, and in encouraging young workers to move into expanding urban areas.

More recently, the housing allowance has grown in favor in some countries because of cost considerations; that is, the per-household cost of a consumer housing subsidy system is substantially less than that of the more traditional producer housing subsidy system, which provided capital grants and interest subsidies to builders and developers. During the last 10 years, the direction of European national housing subsidy policy has been vigorously debated: Should the major accent be put on producer subsidy systems or on consumer subsidy systems?

Two governments—France and Sweden—have shown preference for the consumer approach over the producer approach, and other governments have been increasingly sympathetic to the idea. The scale of housing allowances is fairly impressive. In four countries, approximately one-fifth or more of the total households receive some form of housing allowance, and in three additional countries the figure is approximately one-tenth. Nevertheless, the reality is that as a proportion of total national housing subsidies, consumer subsidies remain secondary. In the seven major countries housing allowances constitute only about one-quarter of the total national housing subsidies.

The seeming contradiction between stated policy preferences and the allocation of housing subsidies is somewhat puzzling. The weight of traditional producer subsidy systems backed by strong producer constituencies could be expected to be important considerations in explaining the contradiction. But several other factors also help explain the weight given to producer housing subsidies. First, notwithstanding periodic statements that housing supply has caught up with housing demand, serious housing shortages have recurred on a regional and local basis and in certain sectors of the housing market. In retrospect, perhaps projections of housing requirements have not taken sufficient account of such factors as higher rates of household formation, higher housing aspirations accompanying rising affluence, and greater dependence on a foreign labor supply.

Second, in light of trade union, religious, and political traditions, there is a special sensitivity to social deprivations attributable to continued local and/or sectoral housing shortages. Hence, there is pressure for a subsidy policy that will ensure the construction of new dwelling units. Third, there seems to be a lack of confidence that even with an adequate housing allowance system the private market will, in fact, meet the remaining unfilled housing needs of certain low-income groups such as the elderly, large families, and immigrant workers and their families. Greater freedom and flexibility in the housing market, particularly with regard to rent regulation, might provide some reason for greater confidence in the private sector.

Unquestionably, affordability has emerged as a major, if not the central, issue in determining a housing subsidy policy. In this respect, primary importance is attached to the housing allowance approach. But, at the same time, there is a strong feeling that as long as housing shortages persist, even on a regional, local, or sectoral basis, producer subsidy programs are essential. Since the cost per household under the producer subsidy system is three to four times higher than under the consumer subsidy system, housing allowances may well continue to be the smaller part of total national housing subsidies among European governments for some time to come. In short, practically speaking, European governments are not opting overwhelmingly for one system or the other. Rather, some kind of mix is the order of the day.

A final central, long-term issue is: Should the housing allowance be folded into a general income maintenance policy on the grounds that the basic problem of the poor is a deficiency of income rather than housing space? At the present stage of social development European governments are resisting the integration of the two systems and are maintaining their housing allowance systems intact for several reasons. First, in many countries, housing inspections accompanying a housing allowance program are believed essential to ensuring that subsidized housing meets minimum housing standards. Second, in promoting and protecting shelter programs, a separate housing allowance is regarded as a more powerful political tool than a general income maintenance policy. Third, a housing allowance system deals more effectively with the housing needs of the working poor than a general income maintenance policy. Fourth, the general view is that there will always be a need for housing programs for households that are not able to afford the costs of that housing.

But whether housing allowance programs ultimately are fully integrated with income maintenance systems or only coordinated with them, there are at least seven specific issues that the two systems need to address and develop in consonance:

- More uniform income definitions;
- more uniform eligibility requirements;
- simpler and more comparable formulas for benefit payments;
- better identification of the needy categories of the population;
- greater program adequacy in coping with poverty;
- preservation and enhancement of work incentives; and
- streamlining of management systems.

The Problem and Its Setting

1

Historical Background

$\mathbf{A}$s the Industrial Revolution swept over Europe, workers were squeezed out of agriculture and drawn to the burgeoning cities. There they became the landless working class quartered in appalling slums that were growing apace. It was a struggle to obtain a roof over one's head.[1]

At the turn of the twentieth century, workers and their instruments of power—trade unions, cooperatives, and political parties—placed slum clearance high on the agenda of essential reforms. Slum eradication was conceived in simple terms.[2] If there were not enough houses, if even those dwelling units which did exist were abominable, and further, if it was great hardship for workers to pay the rents of this housing, then a drastic remedy indeed was required. Only by government financing of large-scale production of low-cost housing through a social housing policy, they contended, would workers obtain decent living conditions.

There are two general ways of subsidizing housing: the producer subsidy system and the consumer subsidy system.[3] In the producer subsidy system the national government finances and builds houses directly and sets rents within workers' ability to pay, or it extends subsidies to another body which produces the house—e.g., a provincial or local government, a non-profit enterprise such as a housing cooperative, or a private firm. These subsidies are generally either direct capital grants, tax concessions, or mortgage loans at subsidized interest rates and are conditional on rents being set at levels that workers can afford. The essential feature of the producer housing subsidy is that public financial assistance goes to the actual producer of the new dwelling unit.

After World War I, the producer housing subsidy grew in popularity, and by the Great Depression of the 1930s, it was being applied in most highly industrialized countries of Europe.[4] World War II intervened, bringing with it disaster for the housing sector—not only in the destruction of existing housing but also in the postponement of new building. As long as the huge housing backlog remained during the early post-World War II period, the producer housing subsidy principle reigned supreme. Producers of housing were pushed to the limit to catch up with housing need. Then, as the pressures of physical shortages began to slacken in the late 1950s and early 1960s, an alternative concept—the consumer housing subsidy—began to surface.[5]

In the consumer housing subsidy concept, government financial assistance generally goes directly to the low-income household that is unable to obtain decent shelter by paying a fair share of its income in rent. With this assistance, the household is able to obtain housing without paying an excessive rent burden. The assistance may be in a regular housing allowance that is applied to the rent or a rent rebate in the case of publicly owned housing. The essential feature is that it is a flexible, personalized payment to the family on the basis of need (as the French say, "a la personne") and not a fixed, general, impersonal, and anonymous subsidy to "bricks and mortar" (or as the French say, "a la pierre").

The first use of the consumer housing subsidy appears to date back to the early 1900s when the Netherlands introduced the principle of a rent subsidy into the Housing Act of 1901. By the beginning of World War I, various Dutch municipalities had granted rent subsidies to families displaced from slums.[6] In the 1930s, Sweden made a housing allowance available to families with children.[7] Finland adopted its first housing allowance system for large families in 1941.

In a burst of wartime social consciousness, in 1943 Australia appointed a Commonwealth Housing Commission to prepare recommendations for the Ministry of Post-War Reconstruction. A comprehensive report presented in August 1944 proposed, inter alia, the adoption of rent rebates for low-income families.[8] The proposal was accepted by the government and incorporated in the Commonwealth and State Housing Agreement in 1945.[9]

After World War II—in 1948—France introduced the housing allowance as a supplement to the family allowance system to assist large families. By the late 1950s and early 1960s, the consumer housing subsidy concept had been incorporated into the national housing policy of a majority of European countries.[10]

NOTES

1. Ernest Ritson Dewsnup, *The Housing Problem in England* (Manchester: University Press, 1907); Harry Barnes, *The Slum: Its Story and Solution* (Hempstead: England Mill Press, 1934).
2. International Labour Office, *European Housing Problems Since the War* (Geneva: International Labour Office, 1924); Edith Elmer Wood, *Housing Progress in Western Europe* (New York: Dutton, 1923).
3. E. Jay Howenstine, *Foreign Housing Subsidy Systems* (Springfield, VA: National Technical Information Service, 1973), Chaps. IV and VII.
4. International Labour Office, *Housing Policy in Europe,* Studies and Reports, Ser. G., No. 1 (Geneva: International Labour Office, 1930).
5. Gunter Schwerz, *Systems and Significance of Individual Subsidization of Accommodation Costs in European Countries* (Bonn: Domus-Verlag, 1966).
6. Hugo Priemus, *Housing Allowances in the Netherlands* (Delft: Delft University Press, 1984), 3.
7. Sweden, Ministry of Housing and Physical Planning, *Housing, Building and Planning in Sweden* (Stockholm: Ministry of Housing and Physical Planning, 1976), 23.
8. Australia, Commonwealth Housing Commission, *Final Report* (Sydney: Ministry of Post-War Reconstruction, 1944), 13.
9. Australia, Ministry for Works and Housing, *Homes for Australia* (Canberra: Ministry for Works and Housing, 1949), 3-5.
10. E. Jay Howenstine, "The Changing Roles of Housing Production Subsidies and Consumer Housing Subsidies in European National Housing Policy." *Land Economics* (February 1975): 86-94.

2

Strategies of Foreign
Housing Allowance Systems

Introduction

Two judgments underlie all housing allowance systems. First, there are large numbers of families that cannot obtain minimum standard housing by paying out a reasonable portion of their income. Second, the most needy households should be accorded first priority in the payment of housing subsidies.

There have, however, been notable differences among housing systems in their approach to the most needy households. For example, there have been different definitions of "most needy," and the principle of the most needy has often been blended with other important economic and social purposes.

For United States policy-making purposes, the strategic role of the housing allowance concept as it has developed in other countries can be best seen by delineating eight rather distinct models of housing allowance systems: large family hardship model; the elderly hardship model; the rent harmonization model; the excessive shelter-to-income model; the tandem–new construction model; the social stability model; the labor mobility model; and the family crisis model.

Large Family Hardship Model

Going back to the turn of the twentieth century when social reformers, trade unions, philanthropic organizations, and religious institutions were rising up against the miseries of urban slums, one of the dominant moral concerns was the welfare of children. How could freedom of opportunity of an enlightened citizenry be assured when children were being reared under wretched living conditions?

The pre-World War II perception was that wages of the working classes were more or less fixed over time. Other things being equal, therefore, an additional child in the family—and in the days before the generalized practice of birth control families tended to be big—led to a worsening of life in two major ways: a smaller portion of family income was available for the consumption of each individual; and each individual had less physical space within the household.

The concern for children found political expression in two ways, i.e., in the establishment of family allowance systems (sometimes called children's allowances) and in social housing programs. Family allowance systems, spearheaded by the International Labour Office created under the League of Nations in 1919, were adopted in most of the highly industrialized countries and provided financial assistance for each additional child in the family to avoid a lowering of standards of living.[1] And social housing (more or less the European equivalent of United States public housing) programs were promoted to eliminate slums.

Since slums could only be overcome by building more housing, it was logical that financial assistance should be in the form of producer subsidies to the builder, that is, mainly to public and nonprofit agencies acting on behalf of the poor. The new social housing was then normally allotted on the basis of a point system to the most needy, which by the nature of circumstances tended to be the largest families.

In the course of time, however, children grow up and leave home, converting large families back to small families. But under the housing regulations of most countries, families were not required to vacate subsidized housing as their level of need changed, e.g., as the size of family shrank or as the level of income rose; rather, they continued to occupy old units indefinitely, even passing them on to the next generation. In this milieu, after World War II, the International Union of Family Organizations (IUFO) became one of the leading protagonists for a housing allowance system based primarily on the large family rationale. It attracted the attention and participation of leading housing experts, and it had an important influence in many countries, especially Belgium, France, Luxembourg, the Netherlands, and Scandinavia.[2]

In the IUFO view, the key to providing adequate succor to the most needy was the development of "individual compensation for housing expenses . . . as closely adapted as possible to the circumstances of the household with children."[3] Such a system would ensure a much more effective use of the existing housing stock on the basis of need. As large families shrank in size and thereby received a smaller housing allowance, they would have an incentive to move to smaller space and to liberate large dwelling units for other growing families.[4]

An important corollary was that housing allowances should operate in a national rental housing market organized on the basis of economic rents rather than in a rent-controlled market stratified on many different rent levels for equivalent accommodations based on differences in past construction costs and producer subsidy systems. This was essential for two reasons. First, it avoided the misuse and waste of housing subsidies on space for families that had low-priority needs or had ceased to be in a needy position altogether, and it encouraged households to move within the market as their housing needs increased or decreased. Second, it stimulated an increase in the supply of rental housing. With the assurance of economic rents, instead of having to compete with low-subsidized rents, private rental housing investors would be encouraged to construct new housing.[5]

The original large family hardship model contained two other concepts, which, although more or less lost in the passage of time, are worth noting. One concerned the formula for calculating the housing allowance. Since the family allowance had become a well-established fixture in national social policy in many countries, it was maintained that the ratio of the family allowance to nonhousing items in the worker's budget provided a ready-made measure of need which could be applied equally well to housing costs. Thus, if the family allowance equaled 20 percent of the nonhousing items in the family budget, the proposal was that the housing allowance should equal 20 percent of the housing cost item in the budget.[6] In countries without such legislation, the IUFO proposed that housing allowances should cover rent in excess of a reasonable percentage of the family income, i.e., between 6 and 12 percent of income depending on the size of the family and its income.[7]

The other interesting concept was that housing space should be measured in terms of its capacity to accommodate people rather than in terms of square meters of floor space or number of rooms. Accordingly, at its 1954 session, the IUFO adopted the concept of a "housing capacity index" based on two criteria: the number of bedrooms and the total number of occupants for these bedrooms. Thus, a dwelling unit with an index—A 4/6—was an apartment of four bedrooms for six persons.[8] This index was believed to be the best possible measure of the housing stock's capacity to meet social need.

Concern for the housing needs of poor large families was prominent in the early evolution of housing allowances. Sweden introduced a housing subsidy for families with many children in the 1930s and has continued to expand the coverage until approximately one-half of all families with children now receive a housing allowance. Finland adopted its first housing allowance system for large families in 1941, the system expanding so that by 1961 it included about 2,000 families.[9] France adopted a housing allowance in 1948 that was payable only to large families which received a family allowance. The Canton of Basle and the city of Zurich in Switzerland launched large family housing allowances in 1963, while Denmark introduced its system for large families and single persons with children in 1964.[10]

Elderly Hardship Model

A second major category of "most needy" households competing for housing subsidies has been the elderly and the physically handicapped. The old-age pension has long been a part of European social security systems; in fact, Bismarck made it a part of the German social insurance system in the 1870s. While fairly comprehensive in coverage, after World War II, European systems were generally deficient in two respects: pensions were relatively small; and, there was little provision for automatically increasing (i.e., indexing) pensions to compensate for increases in costs of living. The systems had been established in an era of price stability, when there was no problem of creeping inflation. As a consequence, a large proportion of the elderly found themselves in a financial squeeze. Although continued rent controls imposed a brake on the rate of increase in shelter costs, periodic relaxation of rent ceilings clearly intensified rent burdens.

The housing allowance concept offered a cogent solution to this problem. It was a simple subsidy for a well-defined, very needy group. Moreover, since the elderly poor were an easily identifiable part of the total poverty problem, governments could provide financial relief without opening the floodgate for massive consumer housing subsidies for all the poor.

In the early development of housing allowance systems, the elderly poor often played a central role. In 1948 France established a rent subsidy system for the aged and the disabled living in old apartments. This subsidy was necessary for persons living on fixed incomes, such as pensioners, to offset rent increases which began to be introduced in the old housing stock. After several amendments, this program was completely overhauled in 1971. Since then it has remained a separate system for the elderly, the physically handicapped, and certain young workers. In 1978, 663,000 elderly persons, 61,600 handicapped individuals, and 81,000 young workers received allowances under this system.

In Sweden, where there are three separate housing allowance systems, municipalities provide a special housing allowance supplementing the national retirement pension when the pension is insufficient to provide an adequate dwelling. Since 1958 the principles governing the subsidy and its financing have been the responsibility of municipalities. As a result, differences in levels of payment prevailed. Means-test rules for determining eligibility have, however, been established by the national government. Beginning in 1982 the government agreed to cover 25 percent of the costs and to coordinate housing allowances for the elderly more closely with the other two more general systems. Among other things, this involved rent ceilings. In 1980, slightly more than one-half of all retired persons—about 800,000—received housing allowances under this system.

Denmark adopted a rent subsidy plan in 1959 specifically for those elderly and disabled persons receiving national pensions that were too small to enable them to obtain adequate unsubsidized accommodations. Eligible persons were required to rent subsidized housing owned by the municipality or a nonprofit or charitable housing association. The housing allowance was paid to the owner, not the renter. Two-thirds of the total costs were financed by the municipality, and one-third was given by the national government. The Canton of Basle (Switzerland) launched a similar program for the elderly in 1963. The Belgian housing allowance system is mainly for the elderly. In Australia, a Supplementary Assistance Plan for rental housing for aged, sole parent, and invalid pensioners was introduced in 1969. Weekly assistance in 1982 was equal to one-half the amount by which rent exceeded $10, with maximum assistance of $10 a week. In December 1982, 417,000 pensioners (or 86 percent of the total pensioners) received Supplementary Assistance for rental housing.[11]

Finland introduced a housing allowance system for the elderly in 1970 to cover housing costs that were above average. The allowance is paid as a part of the national pension system, with the number of recipients rising from 50,000 in 1970 to 179,000 in 1983—or about 50 percent of all housing allowance participants.

The elderly hardship model was adopted by five Canadian provinces— British Columbia, Manitoba, New Brunswick, Nova Scotia, and Quebec—

in the 1970s and 1980s. The aim was to assist the elderly in keeping their existing housing rather than to rehouse them in new projects. The policy reflected the belief that elderly housing generally met acceptable standards and that the problem was one of excessive rent burden.

Elderly recipients appear to predominate in most national housing allowance plans. In fact, historically in France, the Federal Republic of Germany, Sweden, and the United Kingdom, they have constituted from two-thirds to three-quarters of all participants. In other words, housing allowance systems have tended to become a major auxiliary support to old-age pension systems.

European experiences demonstrate that an initial restriction of eligibility to senior citizens (and perhaps handicapped persons) offers an effective political strategy for introducing a housing allowance system. It clearly targets the system to a widely recognized, high-priority category. From a social point of view, the elderly are probably the most highly disciplined sector of the population; thus, the risks of abuses and problems of administration are minimized. Since elderly demographics are generally well known, it is possible to set the lower eligibility age limit at a level that corresponds to the financial resources that the government is ready to make available for such a program. In other words, this approach offers a method for a fine tuning of demand to the current limits of fiscal capacity. If, then, experience demonstrates the practicability of the system, if fiscal capacity grows, and if it is believed appropriate, the age limit can be progressively lowered to embrace a steadily larger part of the population.

Rent Harmonization Model

World War II seriously disrupted the European housing market in many ways, especially the rental housing sector. In the face of wartime inflationary pressures, strict rent controls were applied. After the war, governments were slow to decontrol rents, mainly because of the political risks involved. Consequently, major inequities and distortions arose which even socialists and trade unionists recognized.[12]

First, rent controls created inequities among renters. On the one side, there were the "haves," who—as long-standing tenants—paid excessively low rents; on the other side, there were the "have-nots," such as young couples and war veterans, who paid excessively high rents because they were recent entrants into the housing market. Second, rent controls led to inequities between renters and landlords. Rents often did not cover operating costs, much less yield a fair return on capital invested. Third, rent controls led to widespread physical deterioration in existing housing.

Finally, they were a negative influence on the supply of housing. They were an incentive to convert rental housing to owner-occupancy or commercial use and in certain circumstances to demolish the building and sell the land, and they were a disincentive for new investment in private rental housing.[13]

By the 1960s, although the aim of most European governments was the eventual abolition of rent controls, it had become apparent that piecemeal liberalization would not succeed alone. Consequently, a new concept of "rent harmonization" or "rent equalization" emerged, in which housing allowances had a strategic role to play. The objective was to move systematically toward a single unified rental housing market on an economic cost basis. It was believed that, as a result of rising individual incomes associated with postwar national economic growth and inflation, a majority of tenants could afford to pay higher rents. To avoid hardship for those who had not participated in the prosperity, that is, those who lived on fixed incomes, a housing allowance or rent rebate would be granted.

This melding of policies was highly felicitous. It offered a politically acceptable package by eliminating threatened hardship. It introduced an incentive for families to seek housing space in terms of household requirements rather than because of fortuitously, artificially low rents, and it obtained for the society as a whole a more economic use of the existing housing stock. Moreover, it offered promise of a fair return on capital to landlords, and thus a new capability to keep the rental housing stock in a good state of maintenance and repair.

France appears to have been the first country to link consumer housing subsidies with relaxation of rent controls as an instrument of national policy. In 1948 a modest housing allowance system was introduced to eliminate or at least ease the hardship created for persons on fixed incomes who were not able to cope with rent increases.

In 1955 the Federal Republic of Germany adopted its first housing allowance for similar reasons. The housing allowance was based on the principle that housing expenditures should be kept below 10 percent of the budget for families with very low incomes, rising to 20 percent for those with incomes just under the eligibility limits.

Denmark in 1967 and the Netherlands in 1970 adopted a much more systematic approach. Denmark envisaged the progressive phasing out of rent control over an eight-year period, the Netherlands over a 10-year period. The assumption was that during the previous decade the incomes of most persons had increased sufficiently that they could afford to pay higher rents without exceeding a fair shelter-to-income ratio—in the case of Denmark 20 percent, and in the case of the Netherlands between 13 and 17 percent for families. The housing allowance was an integral part of a rent decontrol policy aimed at easing hardship on households with fixed incomes.

Ireland also followed the principle in 1967 with a differential rent policy that adjusted actual rents to the tenant's income and family circumstances, as rents generally were moved upward toward a more free market level.

In the early 1970s both France and Austria introduced housing allowances to relieve the hardship imposed by increased rents. French legislation limited the application to the elderly and the handicapped. The Austrian 1974 law, applying to low-income families generally, also provided that rent increases should be used to cover proper maintenance and in certain cases improvement costs. In 1973 the Norwegian government increased its housing allowance substantially to mitigate individual hardships that might accompany the relaxation of rent controls and the raising of interest rates on existing mortgages.

Shelter-to-Income Model

Housing is an important item in the family budget. As observed in Chapter 1, the European working class has historically been unable to afford the costs of decent housing. Workers' pre-World War I expectations regarding a decent home and a decent living environment were therefore generally low, or even nonexistent—save through the helping hand of government.

After World War II, however, several factors combined to alter expectations. European economies spurted ahead with rapid technological change, high economic growth rates, and rising individual incomes. During the late 1940s, 1950s, and 1960s, great strides were made in rebuilding destroyed cities and in slum clearance. By the mid-1970s most countries were succeeding in overcoming the global quantitative backlog of housing need, and the "Age of Affluence" was definitely bringing rising expectations to the common man. As a result, two issues began to receive increasing attention, i.e., improving the quality of the housing stock and relieving the excessive shelter-to-income (SIR) burden on low-income families.

The housing allowance is an ideal tool for eliminating excessive rent burdens on poor households. Public policy need only do two things: (1) determine SIRs that various size families can afford to pay,[14] and (2) provide an allowance to cover the difference (or a suitable part of the difference) between actual rents and the maximum percentage of income that families can afford to pay.

This rationale has pervaded several European housing allowance systems, most notably those of Austria, Finland, the Federal Republic of Germany, and the Netherlands. The central principle in the Dutch system is that the tenant should not have to pay more than a reasonable part of his income in rent. In 1978 the standard SIR for the minimum wage earner, that is, the percentage of income which the tenant was deemed capable of paying for rent, was fixed at 11.2 percent. The Finnish system is similar to the Dutch. In 1983 a three-member household at the minimum wage level (i.e., $539–FM 3,000 per month) was expected to pay 14.5 percent of its gross income in rent. The German housing allowance system, covering 1.7 million households or one in every 16 families in 1978, is intended to reduce the burden of housing costs on lower-income households. In Austria, the Housing Promotion Act of 1968 set up a housing allowance system which focused on the financial burdens which lower-income households could reasonably be expected to bear.

Tandem–New Construction Model

During the 1960s and early 1970s, the increasingly high cost of new construction[15] led inevitably to a growing gap between rents for newly built housing and rents for the older housing stock for roughly equivalent accommodations. One of the dire consequences of this gap was that, in spite of persistent housing need, by 1974-75 a large number of dwellings, especially in Denmark, the Federal Republic of Germany, the Netherlands, Sweden, and Switzerland, were remaining vacant for well over a year because rents were more than tenants could afford to pay.[16]

Broadly speaking, governments had three main options. First, they could bring the rents of new housing down to the rent level of the existing housing stock on the assumption that the spurt in housing costs was a temporary aberration that would be corrected with the passage of time. Second, they could bring the rent levels of the old housing stock up to the high levels of the new construction on the assumption that the inflated cost structure was here to stay. Or, third, they could adjust to a continuing gap in sundry middle-of-the-road ways.

In this situation, another housing allowance rationale emerged, which for lack of a better term will be called the tandem–new construction model; this is a housing assistance policy which works as a complementary arm to the national policy on new housing construction. In essence, the housing allowance becomes a tool to facilitate the unloading of new, modern, high-cost apartments on a clientele who could not otherwise afford them.

Norway was a pioneer. In 1967 a national commission was appointed to design a more comprehensive housing subsidy system. One of its central recommendations was that subsidies should be paid only to households living in recently built dwellings; these were the most expensive because of high building costs, high interest rates, and high land costs. But the commission also recommended that subsidies be paid out only for the first 10 years after completion (compared to the then-existing 15-year period), and that during that period, subsidies should be gradually reduced (having in mind possible income and price trends during that period). The commission's rationale relating to new construction was generally accepted in the 1972 housing reform act.

An interesting variation of this model has been developed in Sweden. In 1966, 43 percent of all families with children were living in overcrowded conditions, as legislatively defined, i.e., more than two occupants per room excluding kitchen and living room. Sweden undertook a gigantic effort to upgrade housing quality, using the housing allowance as a means of helping large, low-income families obtain "modern and sufficiently large dwellings." The new system provided an incentive to occupy new, expensive, large dwelling units by offering (within certain broad limits) a 40 percent rent subsidy for the more expensive units, 10 percent higher than that of the less expensive units which received a housing allowance of only 30 percent of the rent.

The tandem–new construction rationale also became an important element in the housing allowance systems of France and the Netherlands.

Social Stability Model

European societies traditionally emphasize social stability. In part this derives from the class structure inherited from the past which looked askance at the instabilities associated with social change. In part it has roots in the strong family, neighborhood, and religious orientations of their urban systems. It may also be partly attributable to the old perception that the size of the national economic pie was more or less fixed and that, consequently, there were fairly well-defined constraints on one's economic well being (that is, until the economic growth milieu that developed after World War II).

In this setting, the eviction of a household because of an inability to pay rent is regarded as a serious threat to social stability: it is disruptive to family life and is a loss to the neighborhood. To diminish this threat, most European countries built into the law considerable tenure rights for renters.

To reduce still further the risk of eviction, a logical next step was to bolster the ability to pay of economically weak households by providing a housing allowance. The elderly have perhaps been among the most vulnerable to circumstances beyond their control. The rent-paying capacity of persons on fixed incomes is rapidly eroded by inflation. Most of the animus of early housing allowance plans for the elderly noted in the Elderly Hardship Model previously discussed appears to have, in fact, been rooted in the concern for social stability. The financial crunch forced elderly persons to give up their homes, and this was regarded as highly inimical to the welfare of those displaced and to the very core of society itself. There is in this respect, therefore, an overlap between the Social Stability Model and the Elderly Hardship Model.

Similarly, low-income families, already suffering hardship from their economic status, are highly vulnerable to forces beyond their control, such as unemployment and depression. To a considerable degree housing allowances in a number of countries have been designed not to improve housing conditions *in situ*, not to enable households to shop around for alternative accommodation, but merely to strengthen the ability of financially weak households to hang on to the housing they have.

Labor Mobility Model

The motif of the labor mobility model is at the opposite extreme of the Social Stability Model. It is the response of a housing market long under the heavy-hand of rent controls.

As observed in the Rent Harmonization Model, there is a strong incentive for households to continue occupying large, low-rent, centrally located apartments long after their housing requirements—as determined by the size of the family—changed because most alternative smaller units are recently built and, therefore, have much higher rents. Socially, this condition is a gross misallocation of housing space. Economically, it constitutes a serious brake on the rate of national economic growth by preventing the labor force from moving easily as economic growth and job markets beckon. To the rescue, at least in part, has come the housing allowance.

The simplest way to use housing allowances as an instrument for promoting labor mobility is to restrict participation to households living in the most recently built apartments, which by definition have incurred the highest costs and are thus let at the highest rents. All countries encountered increasingly difficult problems in finding tenants, particularly among low-income and moderate-income households, to contract for these high-rent units. Going back to its early experience, Sweden limited its housing allowance system established in 1947 to dwellings that were erected or converted after December 1947. Norway restricted its 1972 housing allowance plan to housing built after 1962. The Dutch housing allowance system before 1975 was available only to households living in rental accommodations built after 1960. The two Austrian provinces (Tyrol and

Vorarlberg) and the Danes also provided that households would be eligible only if their accommodation was built after a specified date.

In 1966, in Denmark, the housing problem became a central national issue. In a celebrated Housing Pact worked out by the major Danish political parties, one of the important objectives agreed upon was to encourage greater mobility within the housing stock by means of rent harmonization and the introduction of housing allowances for tenants. Similar considerations have been prominent in French and German housing allowance policies.

An indirect way that governments have applied the labor mobility model is by establishing high standards of physical construction and housing amenities as a condition of participation in the housing allowance system. In many countries only postwar or even more recent vintage construction—and thus the most expensive rental dwelling units—can meet such requirements.

Again the rationale is the same. Rent controls and the basing of rents on postwar construction costs created large rent differentials that may not actually represent real differences in housing habitability. Much of this new postwar construction was in response to economic growth needs, but rent differentials had the unfortunate result of discouraging mobility in the labor market. Encountering difficulties in letting such high-quality, high-rent housing units, governments developed housing allowance systems as a means of reducing the rent burden and providing an incentive for greater labor mobility.

A number of governments, including Denmark, France, the Federal Republic of Germany, the Netherlands, and Sweden, went further and used other types of housing assistance to promote labor mobility. For example, in 1975, the Netherlands adopted a rent readjustment grant to assist households that were capable and desirous of living in better accommodations but who tended to shrink from moving because of the sudden increase in rent and the burden of moving costs. Three types of tenants were eligible: those leaving an older, cheaper unit for a newly built, higher-rent unit ("the moving-up process"); those leaving a slum dwelling for another unit with a higher rent ("slum clearance"); and those living in units that had undergone major modernization and whose rents had been substantially increased ("housing improvement").

Providing the difference in monthly rent was at least $11.86 (FL.30), the Dutch rent readjustment grant covered 75 percent of the difference the first year, 50 percent the second year, and 25 percent the third year. In 1982, the grant was lowered to 60 percent the first year and 40 percent the second year. Certain ceilings were set, however. The tenant's annual 1975 taxable income could not exceed $11,860 (FL.30,000), and the monthly rent of the vacated dwelling could not be more than $98 (FL.250). In addition, a special grant of up to $1,383 (FL.3,500) was available to help cover removal and refurnishing costs for households experiencing major housing improvements or slum clearance and for elderly people moving from low-rent dwellings to smaller, more expensive units or to nonself-contained accommodations.

Family Crisis Model

Frequently low-income and moderate-income families are confronted with temporary household crises, such as loss of a job or ill health of the breadwinner(s), or desertion by the husband or wife. If, because of non-payment of rent, the family is forced to move, this imposes a heavy burden on the household and the community, e.g., loss of local friends and support services, disruption in children's schooling, and the costs of moving. On the other hand, if temporary assistance can be provided, the family can generally resolve the crisis or come to terms with the new situation.

In most countries this kind of crisis is dealt with (if it is recognized) through some form of public assistance. But, in 1981, Victoria Province in Australia embarked on an interesting pilot rental-subsidy program to deal precisely with such situations.[17] The objective is to provide emergency financial support to enable families to remain in their existing situation. The subsidy is temporary and is paid for a maximum period of 12 months. From one point of view, this rationale could perhaps be considered as a subset of the Social Stability Model. But it is sufficiently imaginative in its social and psychological design that it has seemed worthwhile including it as a separate model.

A somewhat related program, the Mortgage and Rent Relief Scheme, was adopted by the Australian government in 1982 to provide assistance to "crisis" cases of people in rental difficulties. The Commonwealth provided the states with $20 million (A$20 million) per annum on a matching basis for three years with the intent of providing short-term assistance (for only about 12 months) until either the crisis was resolved or a longer-term solution was found. Relief was provided in advance as quickly as possible, the first payment being made within two weeks after registration. Changes in household circumstances were identified in the standard quarterly review.[18]

Summary

In foreign experience, the housing allowance has proved to be a highly flexible, versatile tool of national policy. It is an effective means for directly reducing excessive rent burdens on low-income families, especially the elderly, the physically handicapped, and large families, and it also provides powerful support in implementing other important national social and economic objectives. It is an instrument for harmonizing rents and developing unified rental housing markets. It has complemented producer housing subsidy programs by helping to maintain markets for new housing. It has strengthened social stability by assisting financially weak households to hang on to the housing they have. Finally, it is a useful means of stimulating labor mobility needed for national economic growth and new job markets.

The multiple use which governments have made of the various models is shown in Table 1.

TABLE 1
Multiple Uses of Housing Allowance Strategies by Foreign Governments

Model	Countries and Approximate Date of Adoption
1. Large family hardship	Sweden, 1930s France, 1948 Finland, 1962 Switzerland, Basle Canton, 1963; city of Zurich, 1963 Denmark, 1964
2. Elderly hardship	France, 1948 Sweden, 1950s Denmark, 1959 Switzerland, Basle Canton, 1963 Belgium, 1950s Australia, 1969 Finland, 1970 Canadian provincial systems, 1970s
3. Rent harmonization	France, 1948 Federal Republic of Germany, 1955 Denmark, 1967 The Netherlands, 1967 Ireland, 1967 Austria, 1970s Norway, 1973
4. Shelter-to-income ratio	Austria, 1970s Federal Republic of Germany, 1970s Finland, 1970s The Netherlands, 1970s
5. Tandem–new construction	Norway, 1967 Sweden, 1960s France, 1970s The Netherlands, 1970s
6. Social stability	Applied generally
7. Labor mobility	Sweden, 1957 France, 1960s Federal Republic of Germany, 1960s Austria, 1960s Denmark, 1966 The Netherlands, 1970s Norway, 1972
8. Family crisis	Australia, Victoria, 1981

NOTES

1. International Labour Office, *Introduction to Social Security*, third edition (Geneva: International Labour Office, 1984), Chap. 11; *idem.*, *International Survey of Social Security: Comparative Analysis and Summary of National Laws* (Geneva: International Labour Office, 1950), New Ser. No. 23, 21-23; 30-32; 107-9; *see also* Convention 102 adopted by the International Labour Organisation in 1952, "Minimum Standards of Social Security," Part 7, "Family Benefits," International Labour Organisation, *International Labour Conventions and Recommendations, 1919-1981* (Geneva: International Labour Office, 1982), 533-53.

2. Union Internationale des Organismes Familiaux, *Etudes sur le Financement du Logement Familial* (Brussels: Union Internationale des Organismes Familiaux, 1953), 6-26.

3. D. Ceccaldi, "Compensation of Family Housing Expenses" in *Etudes sur le Logement Familial* (Brussels: Union Internationale des Organismes Familiaux, 1955), 25.

4. The IUFO especially stressed the development of systems to promote interchange of dwelling units within the housing stock. Cf. Union Internationale des Organismes Familiaux, *La Mutation des Occupants de Logements dans les Quartiers d'Habitations Sociales* (Brussels: Union Internationale des Organismes Familiaux, 1962).

5. Lucien Wynen, *Le Financement du Logement Social* (Brussels: Union Internationale des Organismes Familiaux, 1962), 2-5.

6. Union Internationale des Organismes Familiaux, *Cout du Logement et Integration du Loyer dans le Budget Familial*, 8th Session, (Brussels: Union Internationale des Organismes Familiaux, 1962), 2; *idem.*, *Compte-Rendu, 8th Session Pleniere* (Brussels: Union Internationale des Organismes Familiaux, 1962), 13.

7. *Idem.*, *Cout du Logement et Integration du Loyer dans le Budget Familial, op. cit.*, 7-8.

8. *Idem.*, *Etudes sur le Logement Familial, op. cit.*, 94-95; *idem.*, *Minimum Habitable Surfaces: Increase in Size and Cost of Dwelling in Relation to the Size of Family* (Brussels: Union Internationale des Organismes Familiaux, 1957).

9. Ossi Paukku, *The Subsidies of the Housing Sector in Finland in 1956-75* (Helsinki: National Housing Board, 1978), published only in Finnish. Information provided by Keijo Tanner, National Housing Board, Helsinki, January 17, 1985.

10. Gunter Schwerz, *Systems and Significance of Individual Subsidization of Accommodation Costs in European Countries* (Bonn: Domus-Verlag, 1966), 9, 19, 43, 51, 59.

11. Tim Field, "Pensioners Who Rent: Problems and Alternatives," *Social Security Journal* (Canberra, June 1983), 25-26; Australia, Department of Social Security, *Annual Report, 1981-82* (Canberra: Department of Social Security, 1982), 62.

12. D. L. Munby, *The Rent Problem* (London: Fabian Publications, 1952), 4-6; Heinz Umrath, "Rent Policy in Western Europe," *International Labour Review* (September 1953), 213-15.

13. E. Jay Howenstine, "European Experience With Rent Controls," *Monthly Labor Review* (June 1977), 21-28.

14. For a more extensive discussion of shelter-to-income ratios among European countries, see Chapter 3.

15. E. Jay Howenstine, *Housing Costs in the United States and Other Industrialized Countries, 1970-1977* (Washington, D.C.: Department of Housing and Urban Development, 1980).

16. A. Andrzejewski and M. Lujanen, *Major Trends in Housing Policy in ECE Countries* (New York: United Nations, 1980), 22.

17. Victoria, Ministry of Housing, *Rental Subsidy Scheme for Families in Crisis* (Melbourne, Victoria: Ministry of Housing, 1981), 8.

18. South Australian Housing Trust, *The Rent Relief Scheme in South Australia: The First Twelve Months* (n.p.: South Australian Housing Trust, 1984), 2-3.

Building a Program

3

Defining Individual Housing Need: Dimensions of a Reasonable Housing Allowance System

Introduction

In most European countries national social policy regards housing as a basic social service, comparable, for example, to education and health. Accordingly, if the family is unable to afford the cost of decent accommodations, the state is deemed to have an obligation to provide housing at a subsidized price. This principle has four main dimensions, all of which involve issues of moral judgment.

First, how much can a family afford to pay? That is, what percent of its income can a family be fairly expected to pay for its housing? Second, at what level of income can a family be reasonably expected to pay the full costs of its housing? Third, what does decent housing cost? That is, what are the essential ingredients in minimum standard housing? Fourth, how much of the gap between the actual rent (for presumably minimum standard housing) and the rent that the family can be expected to pay should be subsidized by the government?

While there is a large area of consensus among governments on these issues, there are also wide differences that are important from a policy viewpoint. This chapter reviews these differences and their rationales.

Shelter-to-Income Ratio (SIR)

The percentage of family income that can be expected to be paid for rent is a highly subjective matter. What might be reasonable in one country or one region at a particular time may be quite different in another country or region, and may in fact change substantially in the same country over a period of time. While no attempt will be made to analyze the social, psychological, economic, and political determinants, several major factors impinging on the concept of *reasonableness* may be noted in a preliminary overview. These observations relate only to highly industrialized countries.

The first factor is the level of economic development: the higher the level of economic development, the higher tends to be the shelter-to-income ratio (SIR); the lower the level of economic development, the lower the SIR. A second closely related factor, and in fact a result of the first factor, is the level of income: the higher the level of income, the higher tends to be the SIR; the lower the level of income, the lower the SIR.[1] These two generalizations have general validity between countries and between families at various income levels within a country. The explanation would seem fairly simple. People in societies with a comparatively low level of economic development and income are forced, as a matter of survival, to spend the bulk of their income on food and clothing. Shelter tends to be low standard, overcrowded, and low cost. As the economic prosperity of the society rises and the minimum essentials of food and clothing are better tended to, there is more leeway in the budget for improvement of shelter. Simultaneously, expectations rise, and the productive capacity of the building industry is growing. As a result, the SIR tends to rise with the increase in the level of economic development and income.

A third factor is the openness and general expansiveness of the society. In societies favored with geographical expanse and abundant natural resources, such as Australia, Canada, and the United States, historically there tends to be a greater accent on individualism, mobility, savings, private property, and capital formation. On the other hand, societies with limited geographical space, such as Western European countries, face land constraints that tend to place greater emphasis on community solidarity, social stability, and social action.

A fourth consideration is the relative importance of the free market. In societies where the market has reigned supreme, shelter tends to be regarded mainly as an individual responsibility. If the family cannot afford decent housing or if the cost of shelter is excessive, that is tough luck; the family—by and large—must care for itself. And in individualistic, open societies with abundant natural resources, historically there has, in fact, been much opportunity for persons to improve their lot through self-help and mutual aid—and incidentally to raise their SIRs. On the other hand, in more closed societies, trade unions and socially oriented groups have organized politically to limit the scope of the free market and to institute comprehensive social policies to protect the working class against abandonment in the free market. If a family cannot afford the cost of decent housing, then it has tended to be viewed as the duty of the state to adopt a social housing program that provides decent housing. Or, if the family actually lives in decent housing but pays an exorbitant rent, then the state tends to be viewed as having a duty to protect the family's standard of living, first by rent controls, and second by providing a housing subsidy that will make for a more reasonable SIR. Viewing the total institutional situation, therefore, it is not surprising to find that in making ethical judgments about what constitutes a reasonable SIR, Western European countries in fact have a lower average SIR and tend to promulgate a lower SIR than is the case in the generally more open societies of Australia, Canada, and the United States.

During the twentieth century there have been considerable changes in the percentage of family income paid for housing in various countries. Before World War II the proportion of family expenditure devoted to rent in Western European countries ranged widely, from 7.7 percent in Austria to 18.9 percent in Switzerland (Table 2). Some adjustments in these data are necessary to express them in terms of SIRs. Family consumption expenditures constitute between 80 and 90 percent of the family income. In statistically measuring family income,[2] taxes, savings, social security payments, and gifts are an addition to consumption expenditures. Thus, if these prewar percentages had been expressed in terms of family income rather than in terms of family expenditures, they would have been lower than indicated in Table 2. If one were to generalize about European pre-World War II experience, it would be fair to say that rents were, on the average, around one-tenth of income.[3]

In non-European industrialized countries, the tradition seems to be different. In Australia, the 1945 Commonwealth and State Housing Agreement established one-fifth as the reasonable proportion of family income that should be paid for rent.[4] Twenty percent also appears to have long been considered an appropriate standard in Canada.[5] In the Canadian public housing program, a sliding scale from 16.7 to 25 percent has been used since 1947. With respect to loans for home ownership in Canada, approved lenders under the National Housing Act increased the proportion of income spent on principal, interest, and taxes from 23 to 27 percent in 1957, and from 27 to 30 percent in 1972.[6] In New Zealand, 25

TABLE 2
Proportion of Family Expenditures Devoted to Rent and Average
Shelter-to-Income Ratios in Industrialized Countries
(Percentages)

Country	Proportion of Family Expenditures Devoted to Rent[1] (One-fifth-general proportion)[2]			Average Shelter-to-Income Ratio		
	Pre-World War II	1947	1953	1960s	1970s	1980s
Australia				—	3.5% of households pay more than 25% (73)[3]; 62% of private renting pensioners pay more than 50% (76)[4]	25% of private rental households pay more than 20% (82)[5]
Austria	7.7 (34)*	—	4.5 (55)	—	—	—
Belgium	11.0 (38)	5.6	7.8	—	—	—
Canada	(20-general standard)[6]	—	—	17 (69)[6]	24% of households pay more than 25% (74)[7]	23.5% (renters-82)[8] 32% of renters pay more than 25% (82)[8]
Denmark	15.1 (31)	8.8	8.1	—	14 (70)[10] 17 (75)[10]	
Finland[11]	16-19 (39-40)[9]	—	—	—	15 (76); 23% of households pay more than 20%	19 (80)[10]
France	8.1 (28)	1.3	3.4	7 (65)[12]	9.5 (70)[12] 9.4 (75)[12]	9.9 (180)[12]
Germany, Federal Republic of	13.1 (36)	—	9.8 20.6	21.9 (60)[13] 22 (65)[13]	21.9 (70)[13] 17.5 (78)[14]	—

Ireland	8.3 (38)	4.8	6.1	7.7 (78)[15]	—
Italy	10.0 (38)	0.5	1.8	—	—
Netherlands, the	11.5 (38)	6.7	5.6	11.35 (79)[16]	15.3 (Renters-81)[17] 14.7 (Owners-81)[17]
New Zealand	(25-general guideline)[18]	—	—	—	—
Norway	12.7 (27-8)	7.2	7.8	—	—
Sweden	11.2 (38-9)	8.4	8.2	—	10 (80)[19]
Switzerland	18.8 (36-7)	—	12.2	14.5% of households pay more than 25% (71)[20]	—
United Kingdom	11.3 (38)	7.6	7.4	11 (78)[21]	—
United States	(20-25- "Rule of Thumb")[22]	—	—	23 (Renters-77)[23] 16 (Owners-77)[23] 28% of households pay more than 25% (74)[7]	Over 50% of very low income renters pay more than 30% (84)[24]

Data from 1973 Australian National Income Survey.

*The numbers in parentheses refer to relevant year.

SOURCES

1. United Nations Economic Commission for Europe, *Financing of Housing in Europe* (Geneva, 1958), 7.
2. Australia: Ministry for Works and Housing, *Homes for Australia* (Canberra, 1949), 5.
3. Australia: Department of Environment, Housing and Community Development, *Housing Allowance Experiment: Final Design* (Canberra, 1978). Vol. 1, 2.
4. Australia: Tim Field, "Pensioners Who Rent—Problems and Alternatives," *Social Security Journal* (Canberra, June 1983), 27; 1976 Census data.
5. Australia: Bureau of Statistics Survey information provided by Warwick Temby, Department of Housing and Construction, January 17, 1985.
6. Canada: Michael Dennis and Susan Fish, *Programs in Search of a Policy* (Toronto, Hakkert, 1972), 58-59.
7. Canada: Paul Burke, Connie Casey, Gerd Doepner, *Housing Affordability Problems and Housing Need in Canada and the United States* (Washington, D.C.: Department of Housing and Urban Development, 1981), 18.

SOURCES (Table 2 continued)

8. Canada: Survey of Consumer Finances, *Statistics Canada*, information supplied by Frances Cameron, Director, Planning Division, Canada Mortgage and Housing Corporation, February 12, 1985.

9. Denmark: Ministry of Housing, *Housing in Denmark* (Copenhagen, 1967), 8. Data from sample survey of skilled and unskilled workers.

10. Denmark: Ministry of Housing, *Human Settlements Situation and Related Trends and Policies* (Copenhagen, 1982), 46. Average expenditure from households' disposable income on housing.

11. Finland: Ministry of the Interior and National Housing Board, *Human Settlements Situation and Related Trends and Policies* (Helsinki, 1982), 40. Actual costs as average of households' disposable income.

12. France: Ministry of City Planning and Housing, *Human Habitation in France: Situation, Tendencies and Policies* (Paris, 1982), 58. Share of rent in household budgets. When data on maintenance of the dwellings, heating, and lighting are included the percentages are as follows: 11.5 (1965); 14.5 (1970); 15.1 (1975); 16.8 (1980).

13. Germany, Federal Republic of: Ministry of Regional Planning, Building and Urban Development, *Current Trends and Policies in the Field of Housing, Building and Planning in the Federal Republic of Germany* (Bonn, 1974), 6. Rent burden of a married male skilled industrial worker with one child on the basis of standard rents.

14. Germany, Federal Republic of: Ministry of Regional Planning, Building and Urban Development, *Monograph on the Human Settlements Situation and Related Trends and Policies* (Bonn, 1982), 57. Data from 1978 housing sample survey of rental sector measuring "cold rent," exclusive of heating costs and other ancillary costs. One-half of households had rents less than 15 percent of income; 15 percent had rents over 25 percent of income.

15. Ireland: Department of the Environment, *Current Trends and Policies in the Field of Housing, Building and Planning* (Dublin, 1980). Data from 1978 Household Budget Survey of average housing expenditures in urban areas devoted to housing expenses, including taxes, mortgage payments, rent maintenance, etc.

16. Netherlands, the: Ministry of Housing and Physical Planning, *Current Trends and Policies in the Fields of Housing, Building and Planning in 1979* (Hague, 1980), 8. Average monthly rent as percentage of "model income."

17. Netherlands, the: Sociaeleen Cultureel Planbureau, *Woonuitgaven 1980–2000: een analyse van mogelijke ontwikkelingen* (Hague, 1984), 22-25; Jan van der Schaar, "Housing Costs in the Netherlands: Trends in the Period 1950–1980 and the Distribution of Housing Costs in 1977," in *Who Will Pay the Housing Bill in the Eighties?*, ed., Hugo Priemus (Delft: Delft University Press, 1983), 35. The percentage of rent in disposable income of a family with two children was 8.3 in old rental housing, 19.7 in new Housing Act rental housing, and 23.6 in new Premium Rental Housing.

18. New Zealand: National Housing Commission, *Housing New Zealand* (Wellington, 1978), 67-68.

19. Sweden: Ministry of Housing and Physical Planning, *Human Settlements in Sweden: Current Situation and Related Trends and Policies* (Stockholm, 1983), 70. Data relate to households comprising two wage earners with two children. A household with one wage earner living in a newly built apartment was 20 percent.

20. Switzerland: Terenzio Angelini and Peter Gurtner, *Marche et Politique du Logement en Suisse* (Berne: Office Federal du Logement, 1978), 84-85. Data collected by a special 1971 study by Publitest, SA, showed that 14.5 percent of households in the rental sector having incomes of less than $411 (SF1,700) per month paid more than 25 percent of their income in rent.

21. United Kingdom: J. B. Cullingworth's comments in *Are Housing Allowances the Answer?*, ed., Janet McClain (Ottawa: Canadian Council on Social Development, 1979), 9.

22. United States: Terry S. Lane, *What Families Spend for Housing: The Origins and Uses of the "Rules of Thumb"* (Washington, D.C.: U.S. Department of Housing and Urban Development, 1977), Chap. 1.

23. United States: Martin D. Levine, *Federal Housing Assistance: Alternative Approaches* (Washington, D.C.: Congressional Budget Office, 1982), 10. Estimates based on the Annual Housing Survey of the U.S. Department of Housing and Urban Development.

24. United States: Samuel R. Pierce, Jr., *Statement at the News Conference and Briefing on HUD's Voucher Program* (Washington, D.C.: U.S. Department of Housing and Urban Development, July 30, 1984). "Very low-income renters" are defined as those with incomes below 50 percent of the median income for their area. In addition, one-quarter of all very low-income renters paid more than 50 percent of their income for shelter.

percent appears to be a general guideline.[7] The "rule of thumb" for housing in the family budget in the United States has been 20 to 25 percent since the nineteenth century.[8] Consequently, the average SIR in the non-European industrialized world appears to have been practically double the European level.

World War II profoundly affected rent burdens. Western European countries, most of which were directly involved in the war, adopted strict rent controls. By the early postwar period, the percentage of family expenditure devoted to rent declined by one-third to one-half, and in two cases—France and Italy—by 1947 declined to 1.3 and 0.5 percent, respectively (Table 2). In such instances shelter almost acquired the status of a free good!

Notwithstanding government efforts to modify and eventually eliminate rent controls, rent regulations continued in some form in most European countries until the present time. In effect, rent controls became an instrument of social housing policy, supplementing national housing subsidies which had not yet reached the level needed to provide social housing for all those who could not otherwise afford decent homes.

Nevertheless, rents in most European countries did rebound in the postwar period. In fact, interestingly enough, during the 1970s, in most European countries, the average rate of rent increase was even faster than that in the United States, although it lagged behind the average rates of increase in building costs, in *per capita* incomes, and in the consumer price index.[9] What is not revealed in these trends, however, is the financial hardship imposed on the minority of renters, particularly low-income and moderate-income households, who were recent entrants in the housing market and who, as a result, were unable to obtain old, low-rent accommodations.

With this broad perspective on SIRs in the industrialized world, it is now appropriate to ask: What is "fair" as applied to the percentage of family income that should be spent on housing? A review of legislative prescriptions reveals a wide variation among governments in their policies concerning this issue (Table 3).

Most governments promulgate a range rather than a single percentage that is reasonable and applicable for households to spend on housing. Two major elements bear on relative household need, the first of which is the level of household income. At very low levels of income, some governments, e.g., France, the United Kingdom, and the Province of Vienna (Austria), place the percentage of income at zero. The belief is that all income is needed for the basic necessities of life, exclusive of shelter. As household income rises above very low levels, in most countries reasonableness is expressed as a progressively higher percentage reaching a max-

TABLE 3
Shelter-to-Income Ratios in Housing Allowance Systems of Industrialized Countries

Country	Lowest Ratio	Average Ratio	Highest Ratio
Australia			
Rent Rebate (45)[1] *	—	20-25	—
Rental Housing Assist. Plan (69)[2]	—	20-25	—
Proposed Demo. Plan (78)[3]	16	20	25
Austria[4]	0 (family of 4 or more persons with monthly income less than $102(AS 2,000-1973)	—	25 (single person household with monthly income over $306(AS6,000-1973)
Canada			
Public Hsg. Program (79)[5]	16.7	Brit. Col. — 30 Manitoba — 25 New Brun. — 30	25
Provincial Systems (81)[6]	—		Nova Scotia — 30 Quebec — 30
Denmark[7]	—	—	15 (81)
Finland (83)[8]	9.4	14.3	15.4
France[9]	0	—	18 (family with 2 children) (77)
Germany, Federal Republic of	7 (66)[10]	17 (79)[11]	22 (66)[10]
Ireland[12]	—	—	Less than one-seventh (78)
Netherlands, the (81)[13]	11.63	—	21.57
Norway (73)[14]	15 (low-income groups)	—	20 (middle-income groups)
Switzerland			
Basle Canton[15]	Depends on no. of children	—	15 (66)
Zurich City[15]	12 (66)	—	15 (66)
Federal Proposal[16]	—	—	25 (71)
United Kingdom[17]	0	—	Variable

United States
EHAP Demonstration Program[18]
Section 8 Program[19]   —   —
Housing Voucher Program (84)[19]

Variable
30
No Limit

—   —

*The numbers in parentheses refer to relevant year.

SOURCES

1. Australia: Ministry for Works and Housing, *Homes for Australia* (Canberra, 1949), 5.
2. Australia: Department of Housing and Construction, *Housing Assistance Act, 1981* (Annual Report for the Year, 1981-82; Canberra, 1983), Chap. 3. Twenty percent is the normal rent-income ratio for tenants in public housing. Tim Field, "Pensioners Who Rent—Problems and Alternatives," *Social Security Journal* (Canberra, June 1983), 27. Twenty percent is also broadly representative of rent-income ratios among provinces for the Supplementary Assistance Allowance for pensioners occupying private rental housing.
3. Australia: Department of Environment, Housing and Community Development, *Housing Allowance Experiment: Final Design* (Canberra, 1978), Vol. 1, 2.
4. Austria: N. Zeyl, "Systems of Individual Subsidies" in United Nations Economic Commission for Europe, Committee on Housing, Building and Planning, *Financing of Housing* (Geneva, 1973), 169-71.
5. Canada: Paul Burke, Connie Casey, Gerd Doepner, *Housing Affordability Problems and Housing Need in Canada and the United States* (Washington, D.C.: U.S. Department of Housing and Urban Development, 1981), 8. The Canadian Task Force on Shelter and Incomes stated that any household whose gross income was below the Low-Income Line, but which was paying in excess of 30 percent of income for housing, has a "relative" affordability problem. Normally, the 25 percent rule is used; but in that particular inquiry 30 percent was used because utilities were included. Task Force on Shelter and Incomes, *Report 1* (Ottawa: Central Mortgage and Housing Corporation, 1976), 12.
6. Canada: Canada Mortgage and Housing Corporation, *Provincial Shelter Allowance Programs* (Ottawa, 1981).
7. Denmark: Information supplied by Hanne Victor Hansen, Ministry of Housing, April 23, 1982.
8. Finland: Keijo Tanner, *The Finnish Housing Allowance System for Families and Single Persons as Applied in 1983* (Helsinki: National Housing Board, 1983), App. 9. The 9.4 percent ratio is for families of eight persons or more; the 15.4 percent for two-person families.
9. France: Ministere de l'Equipement, *La Réforme du Logement* (December-January 1977), 11.
10. Germany, Federal Republic of: Gunter Schwerz, *Systems and Significance of Individual Subsidization of Accommodation Costs in European Countries* (Bonn: Domus-Verlag, 1966), 5.
11. Germany, Federal Republic of: The German Marshall Fund, *Discussion of Housing Policy* (Washington, D.C., 1979), 14.
12. Ireland, Department of the Environment, *A Home of Your Own* (Dublin, 1978), 33.
13. Netherlands, the: Hugo Priemus, *Housing Allowances in the Netherlands* (Delft: Delft University Press, 1984), 56.
14. Norway: Ministry of Local Government and Labour, *Current Trends and Policies Regarding Housing, Building and Planning* (Oslo, 1973), 10.
15. Switzerland: Gunter Schwerz, *op. cit.*, 53, 61.
16. Switzerland: Terenzio Angelini and Peter Gurtner, *Marche et Politique du Logement en Suisse* (Bern: Office Federal du Logement, 1978), 84-85. It is stated that if a household with an income of $411 (SF1,700) per month has to pay more than 25 percent of its income in rent, then that is regarded as "excessive."
17. United Kingdom: J. B. Cullingworth, *Housing Allowances* (1977), 18-19.
18. United States: Office of Policy Development and Research, *Experimental Housing Allowance Program* (Washington, D.C.: U.S. Department of Housing and Urban Development, 1980), 74, 84.
19. United States: Samuel R. Pierce, Jr., *Statement at the News Conference and Briefing on HUD's Voucher Program* (Washington, D.C.: U.S. Department of Housing and Urban Development, July 30, 1984), 9.

imum limit. In the Netherlands there is a long-standing consensus that the tenant should pay not more than one-sixth to one-seventh of his taxable income in rent.[10] The German Housing Allowance Act of 1965 established 7 percent of income as a maximum for very low-income families and 22 percent for those just within the eligibility limits. Denmark established a range of 7.5 to 15 percent. In 1982 a national commission in France recommended that the range should be from 11 to 17 percent, but that in no case should the low-income family pay less than 8 percent.[11]

A second element entering into the concept of fairness is the number of children in the household. In most systems, the maximum percentage of income that should be paid for shelter declines as the number of children increases. For example, at the provincial level in Austria there is wide variation in the concept of reasonableness based on the number of persons in the family. In the case of the lowest income families with four persons receiving less than $102 monthly income (AS2,000), in 1973 Vienna placed the SIR at zero, and five provinces placed the ratio below 10 percent. Salzburg established a 10 percent level, Carinthia a 14 percent minimum, and Burgenland a 20 percent level. However, Burgenland decreased its ratio with the addition of more members, falling to 12.5 percent in families with nine persons.[12]

Defining fairness in variable percentage terms depending on the level of income introduces an important policy issue concerning work incentives: If a person receives a lower housing allowance as his income rises (until a point is reached when the benefit ceases altogether), will this lower his desire to earn additional income and, thereby, affect the labor supply?[13] Describing this phenomenon as equivalent to a "marginal tax rate," Oxley found a significant difference in the British, Danish, and Dutch housing allowance systems. Denmark has a progressive system; in the other two countries the system is regressive, that is, lower "tax rates" are applied at higher-income levels than at lower-income levels.[14] The putative effect of the housing allowance on work incentives is, however, greatly diminished by the fact that in most countries the bulk of the allowances go to persons not in the active labor force, that is, to pensioners and the unemployed. For example, in the Federal Republic of Germany, in 1982, only 25 percent of the housing allowance recipients were employed.[15]

Household Income Ceiling

The second major factor determining the size of the national housing allowance program is the household income ceiling. It is reasonable for financial assistance to be extended to a family when it cannot afford to pay the rent for decent housing; but, when that housing becomes affordable, then it is equally unfair for the taxpayer to support a continued subsidy for that family. At what point, then, does decent housing become affordable to a family?

Practically all governments have established income ceilings for housing allowance participants, but the approach varies considerably. One method is to set a formal income ceiling. The other approach is to establish a ceiling indirectly through the application of other limits.

Some governments created a mathematical cutoff point for eligible households, as the United States did in establishing 80 percent of the area medium income as the ceiling for the housing allowance demonstration program. The Federal Republic of Germany fixed the ceiling at the midpoint in the income distribution; the Australian proposed housing allowance demonstration program set it at 120 percent of national average weekly earnings; in the Netherlands the cutoff is still higher, at the 75th percentile of all income (Table 4). A major advantage of this type of ceiling is simplicity of administration.

In other countries the income ceiling is a more complicated concept and emerges as the overall product of the methods used for calculating the housing allowance. Chief among the factors that influence the income ceiling are family size, size of dwelling, and rents.

Most housing allowance plans take account of family size in calculating the allowance. It is customary for a supplement to be added for each child, sometimes, however, with a limit to the number of eligible children. In Finland the calculation of the income ceiling is exceedingly complex. It is dependent on family size and on the ratio of housing cost to family income. For example, if rent is low, the income ceiling also is correspondingly low.[16] Some countries, including Denmark and the Netherlands, however, establish income ceilings independently of family size.

Within the income ceiling, the subsidy payable is generally determined by the classical approach: the means test. Families are entitled to housing subsidies, i.e., a form of social welfare payments, providing there is proof that they do not have the means to pay the full costs of minimum standard housing. For example, in the Swedish means test, a ceiling is placed on the actual annual income of families eligible to receive a housing allowance. The Swedish plan, as do other plans, takes into account the amount of wealth owned by the claimant. The ceiling, which also considers the number of children and the cost of housing, is raised periodically to compensate for inflation.[17]

The United Kingdom has a more complex approach in its means testing. The national government determines the basic living expenses of the household, called the "needs allowance." This allowance varies according to family size and includes the income tax and national insurance levies

TABLE 4
Income Ceilings as a Condition for Eligibility for Receipt
of Housing Allowances in Industrialized Countries

Country	Annual Ceiling		Criteria for Determining Ceiling	Definition of Income
	Local Currency	U.S. $[1]		
Australia[2] Proposed demonstration	A$13,100(78)*	14,996 (78)	120% of average weekly earnings	Gross income of all household members 16 years and over, including govt. benefits
Austria[3]	AS113,400 (68)	4,362 (68)	Provinces make adjustments taking account of family	Gross household income plus family allowance minus all tax payments
Canada[4]	Manitoba—Elderly (single) C$10,454 (81)	8,719 (81)	—	—
	Manitoba—Family (4 persons) C$13,500 (81)	11,260 (81)	—	—
	Nova Scotia—Elderly (single) C$9,800 (81)	8,174 (81)	—	—
	Quebec—Elderly (single) C$7,200 (81)	6,000 (81)	—	—
Denmark[5]	DK74,500 (81)	10,458 (81)	Ceiling adjusted according to changes in wage rates	Taxable income of all members of household

Country				Income definition
Finland[6]	FM108,240 (4 persons) (83)	19,432 (83)	Function of rent, income, and family size	Taxable income of all household members and gross income of all household members
France[7]	FF32,640 (72)	6,471 (72)	—	Taxable income; assumed to be 72% of gross income of worker
Germany, Federal Republic of[8]	DM22,320 (78) (4 persons)	11,112 (78)	Mid-point in income distribution[9]	Gross income of all members of family, minus standard deduction of 30%
Netherlands, the[10]	FL39,000 (83)	13,665 (83)	75th percentile of all incomes; ceiling revised every year in light of changes in rents and incomes[11]	Taxable income
Norway[12]	NK45,000 (72) (4 persons)	6,830 (72)	Function of family size and rent ceiling	—
Sweden[13]	SK75,000 (82) (4 persons)	11,938 (82)	Function of family size and cost of dwelling	Taxable income
United Kingdom	£3,900 (77)[14] (no prescribed ceiling but operationally)	6,807 (77)	"Reckonable income"[15]	Aggregate gross household income, plus 0.1% of any uninvested capital[15]
United States EHAP Program[16]	(4 persons—Phoenix)	8,650 (73)	80% of area median income	—
Section 8 Prog.[17]	—	—	80% of area median income	—
Housing Voucher (84)[18]	—	—	50% of area median income	—

*The numbers in parentheses refer to relevant year.

TABLE 4 (continued)

Note: Contemporary annual exchange rates published by International Monetary Fund used for converting local income ceilings into U.S. dollars.

SOURCES

1. Local currency prices converted by then-existing exchange rates published in International Monetary Fund, *International Financial Statistics Yearbook, 1983* (Washington, D.C., 1984).

2. Australia: Department of Environment, Housing and Community Development, *Housing Allowance Experiment: Final Design* (Canberra, 1978), Vol. 1, Sec. 12, 53.

3. Austria: N. Zeyl, "Systems of Individual Subsidies" in United Nations Economic Commission for Europe, Committee on Housing, Building and Planning, *Financing of Housing* (Geneva, 1973), 154, 172.

4. Canada: Canada Mortgage and Housing Corporation, *Provincial Shelter Allowance Programs* (Ottawa, 1981).

5. Denmark: Information supplied by Hanne Victor Hansen, Ministry of Housing, April 23, 1982.

6. Finland: Keijo Tanner, *The Finnish Housing Allowance System for Families and Single Persons in 1983* (Helsinki: National Housing Board, 1983), 2-3.

7. France: Ministere de l'Equipement, *La Réforme du Logement* (December-January 1977), No. 103, 9; N. Zeyl, *op. cit.,* 155.

8. Germany, Federal Republic of: Ministry for Land Development, Construction and Urbanization, *Rent Allowance: 1978* (Germantown, MD: HUD USER, 1977), 7.

9. Germany, Federal Republic of: Forma Consulting Co., *A Brief Review of the International Experience with Housing Allowances* (Ottawa: Canada Mortgage and Housing Corporation, 1978), 10.

10. Netherlands, the: Hugo Priemus, *Housing Allowances in the Netherlands* (Delft: Delft University Press, 1984), 56.

11. Netherlands, the: Forma Consulting Co., *op. cit.,* 10.

12. Norway: N. Zeyl, *op. cit.,* 155.

13. Sweden: The Swedish Institute, *Fact Sheets on Sweden* (Stockholm, August 1982), 1.

14. United Kingdom: Forma Consulting Co., *op. cit.,* Annex, 3.

15. United Kingdom: J. B. Cullingworth, *Housing Allowances: The British Experience* (Toronto: Centre for Urban and Community Studies, University of Toronto, 1977), 18-19.

16. United States: Office of Policy Development and Research, *Experimental Housing Allowance Program* (Washington, D.C.: U.S. Department of Housing and Urban Development, 1980), 99.

17. United States: Martin D. Levine, *Federal Housing Assistance: Alternative Approaches* (Washington, D.C.: Congressional Budget Office, 1982), 27.

18. United States: Samuel R. Pierce, Jr., *Statement at the News Conference and Briefing on HUD's Voucher Program* (Washington, D.C.: U.S. Department of Housing and Urban Development, July 30, 1984), 8.

paid by an employed person. It may be roughly considered as the subsistence level. A tenant whose "reckonable income" (i.e., gross income including the spouse's income) equals the needs allowance receives a housing allowance equal to 60 percent of the eligible rent. However, where the tenant's income is less than the needs allowance, the rent is reduced at a rate of 25 percent of the amount that it falls below the needs allowance, finally reaching zero. For tenants whose incomes exceed the needs allowance, a percentage of this (i.e., 17 percent) is added to the minimum rent.[18]

The methods of computing income for income ceiling purposes vary considerably. The most widely used definition of income for housing allowance purposes is taxable income. This has the simplicity of taking an already determined figure that enjoys wide acceptance. Some governments simplify the process still further by establishing a fixed percentage deduction from gross income. Thus France has defined taxable income as 72 percent of the worker's gross income, while the Federal Republic of Germany provides for a flat deduction of 30 percent from the cash income of all members of the family.

The other concept of income used by governments is gross household income. Starting with aggregate gross household income, the United Kingdom makes minor adjustments by adding 0.1 percent of any uninvested capital exceeding $450 (£300), and by subtracting certain forms of income such as disability pensions or industrial accident payments. Austria adds family allowance payments to gross household income and then subtracts all tax payments. In the proposed Australian housing allowance plan, household income is defined as the gross income of all household members 16 years and older, including various kinds of government benefits.

The persistence of inflation during the last 10 years has posed certain problems of equity in the coverage of housing allowance systems. If income ceilings governing housing allowance eligibility are raised, *pari passu*, with the rate of general inflation in the economy, then the level of participation remains basically unaffected. But if ceilings are not raised commensurate with the rate of inflation, then each year a certain number of housing allowance recipients will be automatically dropped from the system even though relatively their needs remain undiminished. This on-again, off-again participation results in substantial hardship to needy families, and is costly and cumbersome administratively.

To deal with the above problem, some governments, e.g., the Netherlands, built an automatic adjustment mechanism into the basic legislation by specifying that each year a new ceiling shall be established in the light of current changes in wages and prices. When the number of applicants increased sharply in the early 1980s as a result of increasing rents and stagnating incomes, the government lowered the income ceiling to limit the growth of the housing subsidy budget.[19] This resulted in relative stability in the number of persons protected by housing allowances.

Rent Ceiling

The third major factor in developing a reasonable housing allowance system is the economic cost of minimum-standard housing. On the one hand, in principle, the allowance should be sufficiently large so that the recipient can pay the rent of at least minimum-standard housing; but, on the other hand, it should not be so large that the recipient is able to obtain what might be described as luxury housing.

As indicated in Chapter 4, "Physical Structure," most housing allowance systems require that recipients live in accommodations that meet minimum physical standards. Since what constitutes "minimum" is constantly evolving, and since building costs have been continually rising in the postwar period, the cost of minimum-standard housing has not been a fixed, determinable amount. The most widely used guide in establishing rent ceilings, therefore, has been the average rent in the housing market area. The average level (whatever it may be) carries a certain moral connotation giving it an aroma of reasonableness and a quality of acceptability (Table 5).

The proposed Australian housing allowance plan established maximum rent levels that reflected "adequate accommodation in an average suburb, depending on the size and basic needs of the families." Following a given formula, the required number of bedrooms was determined by the size of the family and the age and sex of its members. The rent ceiling was, in turn, established according to the number of bedrooms needed. The dollar amount for the various levels of maximum rent was then set on the basis of results of rental surveys conducted at regular intervals.

In the United Kingdom the rent ceiling is linked implicitly, though not formally, to the concept of "fair rents," which was introduced in the 1965 Rent Act in relation to the private sector. Fair rents were defined as the likely market rent that a dwelling could command if supply and demand for rented accommodations were broadly in balance in the area concerned. Although British law has not stated that the ceiling should be the "fair rent" level in a particular housing market, a maximum rebate allowance has been established presumably with a fair rent level in mind. It is to be noticed, however, that the British Secretary of State has the power to authorize higher allowances in an area where rents are "exceptionally high." In 1976 there were 14 local authorities. all in Greater London, which had such authorizations.[20]

In Canada, the maximum rent under the rent supplement program is a comparable market rent as determined by the Canada Mortgage and Housing Corporation. In all the Canadian provincial housing allowance plans, mainly for the elderly, dollar rent ceilings have been set, e.g., ranging for a single person in 1981 from $150 (C$180) a month per person in Quebec to $204 (C$245) a month in Nova Scotia. It is implied, although not formally stated, that these rents are sufficiently high to obtain minimum-standard housing for the occupants (whatever that might consist of).

Denmark, France, and Norway adopted a similar policy. In 1973 the rent ceiling in Denmark was around $240 (DK1,500) monthly; in France, in 1973, for a two-person household without dependents it was around $48 (FF215) for pre-1948 rented buildings and around $67 (FF300) for post-1948 rented buildings; in Norway, in 1973, it was around $123 (NK708) monthly, rising with the number of persons in the household.

The United Kingdom, as observed above, established 40 percent of the rent as a norm that the average low-income household should pay for shelter. This minimum is, however, reduced to zero in the case of very poor families. Similarly in the original French housing allowance system, the minimum rent in 1973 was zero if the monthly household income fell below $123 (FF620) a month.

The Federal Republic of Germany has a complex system for determining average rents. The allowable cost of accommodation, i.e., the equivalent of average rent, is deemed to be the lesser of: (1) actual rent paid, or (2) an amount based on the size and age of the dwelling, the size of the community in which the house is located, and the facilities within the house.

In Canada, a Task Force on Shelter and Incomes recommended that two-thirds of the median rent paid in each province be used as the "minimum rent" or the norm. The Task Force maintained that a provincial, rather than a national, norm should be used because welfare assistance is determined at the provincial level, and there are substantial variations in income levels and rents among provinces. The Task Force believed that a housing allowance should be paid only where housing market conditions were "abnormal," that is, where exceptionally high rents prevailed.[21] The provinces would then be free to choose whether to set a maximum market rent.

Another aspect of the rent structure that enters into the realm of "reasonableness" is the concept of a "minimum rent" which must be paid before a household is eligible to receive a housing allowance. The rationale is that each individual has a moral obligation to make some

TABLE 5
Rent Ceilings in Housing Allowance Systems in Industrialized Countries

Country	Monthly Ceiling		Criteria for Determining Ceiling	Method of Measurement
	Local Currency	U.S. Dollars[1]		
Australia Rental Hsg. Assist. Plan[2]	Average 2-bedroom, metropolitan apartment range: A$150 (Tasmania)—A$260 (N.S. Wales) (84)*	126-218 (84)	80% of market level[3]	—
Proposed Demonstration Plan[4]	—	—	Rent level for adequate accommodation in average suburbs, depending on size and basic needs of family	Special rent surveys based on bedrooms required as follows: (1) one bedroom for each couple; (2) one bedroom for each person, 18 or over; (3) one bedroom for two persons aged 10 to 17 of same sex; (4) one bedroom for two persons under 10; and (5) special arrangements if persons 10 to 17 of different sex
Austria[5]	Variable	—	Space ceiling: 50 square meters 1 person; 20m[2] for each additional member; maximum of 150m[2] for families with more than four children	—

Country	Amount	Value	Basis	Notes
Canada[6]	British Columbia C$205 (single); C$225 (couple) (81)	170(81)	—	—
	Manitoba C$240 (single); C$270 (couple) (81)	200 (81)	—	—
	Nova Scotia C$245 (single); C$320 (couple) (81)	204 (81)	—	Rent paid for fully serviced accommodation, including heat
	New Brunswick C$175 (single); C$200 (couple) (81)	145 (81)	—	
	Quebec C$180 (single); C$200 (couple) (81)	150 (81)	—	—
Denmark[7]	DK1,500 (73)	248 (73)	Concept of residual rent to be borne by all households	—
Finland[8]	FM 1809 (4 persons) (83) Variable	325 (83)	Household size, floor space, equipment, location, construction age	Depends mainly on (1) reasonable floor space (square meters) according to family size, (2) maximum rent per square meter of floor space
France[9]	FF215 (pre-1948 building) (73) FF300 (post-1948 building) (73) FF800 (APL Program) (77)	48 (73) 67 (73) 163 (77)	Minimum rent concept: family must pay at least minimum	—
Germany, Federal Republic of[10]	DM550 (4 persons) (78)	274 (78)	Ceiling varies according to date of construction, amenities, size of locality and family composition	—
Netherlands, the[11]	FL650 (84)	197 (84)	—	Dwelling completed after 1971; in city over 500,000; with collective heating and with bath or shower

TABLE 5 (continued)

Country	Monthly Ceiling		Criteria for Determining Ceiling	Method of Measurement
	Local Currency	U.S. Dollars[1]		
Norway[12]	NK708 (couple) (73)	123 (73)	—	—
	NK833 (5 persons) (73)	144 (73)	—	—
Sweden[13]	SK1,000 (4 persons) (82)	159 (82)	—	—
United Kingdom[14]	Variable: No ceiling prescribed but operationally £63 (London) (77)	110 (77)	"Eligible rent"; "problem of administrative discretion"	—
United States	EHAP: Demand Exp.—Phoenix—4 pers.	190 (75)[15]	No ceiling	—
	EHAP: Supply Exp.—Brown Cty—4 pers.	220 (79)[15]	No ceiling	—
	Sec. 8 Prog. (Urban—Average gross rent)	243 (80)[16]	Fair market rent	—

*The numbers in parentheses refer to relevant year.

SOURCES

1. Local currency prices converted at the then-existing exchange rate. International Monetary Fund, *International Financial Statistics Yearbook 1983* (Washington, D.C., 1984).
2. Australia: Information provided by Warwick Temby, Department of Housing and Construction, January 17, 1985.
3. Australia: Department of Housing and Construction, *Housing Assistance Act, 1981: Annual Report for the Year, 1981-82* (Canberra, 1983), 25.
4. Austria: Department of Environment, Housing and Community Development, *Housing Allowance Experiment: Final Design* (Canberra, 1978), Vol. 1, 5.
5. Austria: N. Zeyl, "Systems of Individual Subsidies" in United Nations Economic Commission for Europe, Committee on Housing, Building and Planning, *Financing of Housing* (Geneva, 1973), 161.
6. Canada: Canada Mortgage and Housing Corporation, *Provincial Shelter Allowance Programs* (Ottawa, 1981).
7. Denmark: N. Zeyl, *op. cit.,* 156, 158.
8. Finland: *The Finnish Housing Allowance System for Families and Single Persons as Applied in 1983* (Helsinki: National Housing Board, 1983), 3, App. 1, par. 4.
9. France: Ministere de l'Equipement, *La Reforme du Logement* (Paris), December—January 1977, 9; N. Zeyl, *op. cit.,* 158.
10. Germany, Federal Republic of: Ministry for Land Development, Construction and Urbanization, *Rent Allowance: 1978* (Germantown, MD: HUD USER, 1977), 10.
11. Netherlands, the: Information supplied by Hugo Priemus, Professor of Housing, Delft University, January 2, 1985.
12. Norway: N. Zeyl, *op. cit.,* 158.
13. Sweden: Housing Subsidy Committee, *Housing Subsidies* (Germantown, MD: HUD USER, 1982), 11-12.
14. United Kingdom: J. B. Cullingworth, *Housing Allowances: The British Experience* (Toronto: Centre for Urban and Community Studies, University of Toronto, 1977), 18-19, 21.
15. United States: Office of Policy Development and Research, *Experimental Housing Allowance Program* (Washington, D.C.: U.S. Department of Housing and Urban Development, 1980), 89-99.
16. United States: Abt Associates, *Participation and Benefits in the Urban Section 8 Program* (Washington, D.C.: U.S. Department of Housing and Urban Development, 1981), 356.

kind of rent payment—even though it may be only a token amount—before the person is entitled to receive housing assistance. Denmark has a concept of "residual rent" which must be borne by all households.

The new French housing allowance system (l'Aide Personnalisee au Logement) provides that each household must pay a rent in excess of a "minimum rent," which is a variable amount based on income and family composition. Similarly, Norway grants a housing allowance on condition that the household makes a minimum annual expenditure for shelter; in 1973 the annual minimum for a one-person household was around $277 (NK1,600), rising to around $520 (NK3,000) for households of five persons or more. The Finnish system incorporates an implicit minimum rent concept. Varying according to family size and income, minimum rent in 1983 was equal to the smallest amount of housing allowance payable (that is, $12 [FM66] per month) plus the reasonable amount of rent which the household should pay (derived from the shelter-to-rent ratio).[22]

Unaffordable Gap to Be Covered by Subsidy

Having determined the size of the gap between what a family can afford to pay and what minimum-standard housing costs, the final question is: What part of the gap should be covered by government subsidy, and on what terms (Table 6)? The answers to these questions are first of all moral in nature, and secondly, financial.

From the moral point of view, it can be argued that the government should pay 100 percent of the gap. Otherwise the cost of shelter exceeds what the family can afford to pay, with the result that vital elements in its standard of living must be sacrificed in order to make rent payments. This could be regarded as morally wrong.

At the same time, it is not necessarily reasonable to expect the government to cover, without qualification, 100 percent of the gap between the actual rent and the rent which the family can afford. It would not be generally regarded as a moral duty of government to underwrite above minimum-standard housing (or luxury housing) for households receiving incomes below the poverty line. Moreover, paying all the gap would encourage families to overconsume housing services (that is, to occupy higher quality accommodations than is required to meet minimum needs); this could be regarded as a wasteful use of scarce resources. Such a policy might also violate the principle of horizontal equity; that is, families of the same income and size could be consuming housing of different qualities at the same cost to themselves. On the other hand, some arrangement to divide the cost of the gap between the government and the household creates an incentive for the participant not to rent the most expensive unit offered in the market.

TABLE 6

Percentage of Gap Between Actual Rent and What the Household Can
Afford to Pay Covered by Foreign Housing Allowance Systems
(Percentages)

Australia	
Tenants in Public Housing[1]	100
Tenants in Private Rental	
Housing-Supplementary	
Assistance Plan[2]	50
Proposed Demonstration[3]	3 Models: 64; 80; and 100
Austria[4]	100 ("the difference between the actual and the reasonable housing expenses")
Belgium[5]	20-50 percent reduction in rent for large families depending on number of children
Canada[6]	
British Columbia	75 percent of difference above 30 percent of income within maximum
Manitoba Elderly Plan	90 percent of difference above 25 percent of low-income range within maximum
Manitoba Family Plan	Up to 90 percent of difference above 25 percent of high-income range within maximum
Nova Scotia	50 to 75 percent of difference above 30 percent within maximum
Quebec	75 percent of difference above 30 percent within maximum
Denmark[7]	
Pensioners Plan	100
Nonpensioners Plan	75
Finland[8]	
General Plan	80 percent of the difference between the approved rent (including heating costs) and the reasonable rent
Pensioner Plan	85
France[9]	60-85; depends on family income, number of children, and a legislatively determined coefficient
Germany, Federal Republic of[10]	Variable; depends on family income and number of children
Ireland[11]	100
Netherlands, the[12]	100 for minimum wage workers; no less than 65 for higher income workers
Norway	
Elderly Plan[13]	80
Nonelderly Plan[14]	65
Sweden[15]	Up to 80
Switzerland (Basle Canton)[16]	10-40, plus an extra allowance ranging from 20 to 40 percent of shelter costs which exceed 20 percent of family income
United Kingdom[17]	60 percent of eligible rent when income equals needs allowance
United States	
Section 8 Program	100
EHAP Program[18]	Variable
Housing Voucher[19]	Variable

TABLE 6 (continued)

SOURCES

1. Australia: Department of Housing and Construction, *Housing Assistance Act, 1981: Annual Report for the Year, 1981-82,* (Canberra, 1983) 25 ff.
2. Australia: Tim Field, "Pensioners Who Rent—Problems and Alternatives," *Social Security Journal* (Canberra, June 1983), 25.
3. Australia: Department of Environment, Housing and Community Development, *Housing Allowance Experiment and Final Design* (Canberra, 1978), Vol. 1, 4, 11-13.
4. Austria: Ministry of Construction and Technology, *Tendencies and Policies in the Field of Housing, Building and Planning* (Vienna, 1973), 3.
5. Belgium: Ministry of Public Health and Family Welfare, *Social Housing Policy in Belgium* (Germantown, MD: HUD USER, 1984), 57. Translation of Belgium Ministry of Public Health and Family Welfare monograph (Brussels, 1969).
6. Canada: Canada Mortgage and Housing Corporation, *Provincial Shelter Allowance Programs* (Ottawa, 1981), 6.
7. Denmark: Information supplied by Hanne Victor Hansen, International Relations Division, Ministry of Housing, April 23, 1982.
8. Finland: Keijo Tanner, *The Finnish Housing Allowance System for Families and Single Persons as Applied in 1983* (Helsinki: National Housing Board, 1983), 8.
9. France: Ministere de l'Equipement, *La Reforme du Logement* (December—January 1977), 8-9.
10. Germany, Federal Republic of: Ministry for Land Development, Construction and Urbanization, *Rent Allowance: 1978,* and *idem., Rent Allowance and Rent Report* (Germantown, MD: HUD USER, 1977). Translation of German reports.
11. Ireland: Department of the Environment, *A Home of Your Own* (Dublin, 1978), 33. The differential rent system provides for minimum weekly rent of around $1 (10 pence); in all cases the tenant pays less than one-seventh of assessable household income in rent. The local authority pays the difference between the economic rent and what the tenant can afford to pay. The average weekly rent paid on a new local authority house was $8.63 (4.50 Irish pounds—1978); the average weekly subsidy was $51.82 a week (27 Irish pounds—1978).
12. Netherlands, the: Hugo Priemus, *Housing Allowances in the Netherlands* (Delft: Delft University Press, 1984), 56.
13. Norway: Ministry of Local Government and Labour, *Current Trends and Policies in the Field of Housing, Building and Planning* (Oslo, 1978), 8.
14. Norway: N. Zeyl, "Systems of Individual Subsidies" in United Nations Economic Commission for Europe, Committee on Housing, Building and Planning, *Financing of Housing* (Geneva, 1973), 181.
15. Sweden: K. F. Watson, F. Ermuth, and W. Hamilton, *A Comparative Analysis of Housing Allowance Programs* (Ottawa: Central Mortgage and Housing Corporation, 1978), F19-20.
16. Switzerland: Gunter Schwerz, *Systems and Significance of Individual Subsidization of Accommodation Costs in European Countries* (Bonn: Domus-Verlag, 1966), 53-54.
17. United Kingdom: J. B. Cullingworth, *Housing Allowances: The British Experience* (Toronto: Centre for Urban and Community Studies, University of Toronto, 1977), 19.
18. United States: Office of Policy Development and Research, *Experimental Housing Allowance Program* (Washington, D.C.: U.S. Department of Housing and Urban Development, 1980), 73.
19. United States: Samuel R. Pierce, Jr., *Statement at the News Conference and Briefing on HUD's Voucher Program* (Washington, D.C.: U.S. Department of Housing and Urban Development, July 30, 1984), 9.

Looking at the real world situation, i.e., the actual condition of the housing stock available to and inhabited by most low-income families in most highly industrialized countries, the above observations may be largely academic. As evidenced by the census of 1970-71, a considerable part of the European housing stock does not yet meet generally regarded minimum housing standards (Table 7). Nevertheless, if low-income families choose to live in above-minimum-standard housing, then it could be

TABLE 7
Percentage of Dwellings Equipped with Basic Facilities
in European Countries, 1970–1971

Country	Piped Water	Lavatory	Fixed Bath or Shower
Austria	84.2	69.8	52.9
Belgium	88.0	50.4	47.8
Bulgaria[1]	66.1	28.0	34.0
Czechoslovakia	75.3	49.0	58.6
Denmark	98.7	90.3	76.5
Finland	72.0	61.4	39.0[2]
France[3]	90.8	51.8	50.2
German Democratic Republic	82.1	40.9	38.7
Federal Republic of Germany[4]	99.2	84.0	81.8
Greece	64.9	41.2	35.6
Hungary	36.1	27.2	31.7
Ireland	78.2	69.2	55.4
Italy	86.1	79.0	64.5
Netherlands, the	—	80.8	81.4
Norway	97.5	69.0	66.1
Poland[5]	55.1	40.7	38.2
Portugal	47.8	33.7	32.6
Spain	70.9	70.9	46.4
Sweden	97.4	90.1	78.3
Switzerland	—	93.3	80.9
United Kingdom	98.3[6]	86.3	90.7
Yugoslavia	33.6	26.2	24.6

Notes: 1. 1975.
        2. Excluding saunas.
        3. 1968.
        4. 1972.
        5. 1974.
        6. 1961.

Source: A. Andrzejewski and M. Lujanen, *Major Trends in Housing Policy in ECE Countries* (Geneva: United Nations Economic Commission for Europe, 1980), 16. Drawn from United Nations Economic Commission for Europe, *A Statistical Survey of the Housing Situation in the ECE Countries Around 1970* (New York, 1978).

morally argued that the subsidy rate for that portion which is above the average rent or above minimum-standard housing should be less than 100 percent.

Turning now to the financial side of the issue as to what part of the gap the subsidy should cover, there are both economic and political considerations. From an economic point of view, the question concerns the size of the gross national product (GNP) and the rate of national economic growth. Are GNP and the economic growth rate sufficiently high that the economy can afford the level of housing subsidies required to pay 100 percent of the gap? If the answer is yes, then there are no economic limits. But, if the answer is no, then economic considerations counsel that governments should cover only a part of the gap. Since there are no well-defined limits to taxable capacity among nations, the economic aspect of the problem admits no simple definitive solution.

The political aspect is perhaps even more indeterminant. It concerns the degree of commitment which the citizenry is willing to make to assist low-income households. Several governments cover 100 percent of the gap.

The Australian rent-rebate program adopted in 1945 was novel. The basic principle was that if a public housing tenant's "economic rent" (which covered "normal provision for outgoings on the property, such as capital repayment, interest, taxes, maintenance, etc.") exceeded one-fifth of the family income, the difference would be made up by a rent rebate. The program covered 100 percent of the gap when the family income was equal to the basic wage. If because of sickness or unemployment the family income was less than the basic wage, the rebate was increased by one-quarter of the amount by which it was less than the basic wage. But if the family income was more than the basic wage, then the rebate was decreased by one-third of the amount by which it exceeded the basic wage. In any case, the rent rebate could not be so great that it brought the rent below the minimum level established for invalid and old-age pensioners.[23] It may also be noted that the 1978 proposed Australian housing allowance experiment aimed to test consumer reaction to three principal levels of subsidizing the gap, i.e., at 100 percent, 80 percent, and 64 percent.

In Austria the housing allowance covers the difference between the actual rent and a reasonable rent, taking into account the level of income, the size of family, and the percentage of household income deemed a reasonable allocation of costs. There does not seem to be any inquiry as to whether the actual accommodation rented is higher than the minimum-standard level.

Pensioners in Denmark have enjoyed a favored status for many years. The government pays 100 percent of the differential between the actual rent and the reasonable rent which the household must pay. Thus, in 1979, a pensioner within the annual income ceiling of $14,160 (DK74,500) had to pay 15 percent of his income, i.e., $944 (DK4,966), toward his shelter cost. If the actual rent was more than $944, the housing allowance covered 100 percent of the differential. By contrast, nonpensioners receive only 75 percent of the differential, having been raised to this level from 66 percent in 1967.

The Dutch government, in a major 1975 reform affecting workers earning the minimum wage, assumed responsibility for 100 percent of the differential between the actual rent and 11.35 percent of the monthly income of the worker. The percentage of the gap, for which the government is responsible, declines as the worker's income rises, but it is in no case less than 65 percent.

On the other hand, a number of governments have not been ready to assume 100 percent of the gap between actual rents and what is regarded as a reasonable rent that low-income households can pay. Several governments cover roughly three-fourths of the gap, particularly for the elderly. The Canadian provincial programs in British Columbia, Manitoba, Nova Scotia, and Quebec pay from 50 to 90 percent of the difference between the actual rent and 25 to 30 percent of total income up to maximum rent levels. In Norway, gap coverage for the elderly increased in 1971 from 70 to 80 percent of the differential between actual and reasonable housing expenditures, although for the nonelderly the percentage remained at 65 percent.

Sweden covers a portion of the gap between the actual and the reasonable rent up to a maximum of 80 percent for the lowest income household, i.e., households without children in 1977 with annual incomes of less than $7,140 (SK32,000). For households with income above the minimum, the amount of the housing allowance is reduced according to a progressive formula. The housing allowance granted by the Finnish National Housing Board through local authorities covers 80 percent of the gap between approved rent and a reasonable rent that the householder should pay. The National Housing Society in Belgium provides a 20 to 50 percent reduction in rent to large families depending on the number of children.

In the Federal Republic of Germany, the original objective of the housing allowance system was to pay the full differential between so-called "bearable" housing costs and actual costs. But this concept was rejected for two reasons.[24] First, without a rent ceiling households of equal income and family size could consume housing of widely different qualities at the same cost to the family. This violated the principle of horizontal equity, i.e., equity among families at the same income level. Second, in the long-run it would lead to an unbearable fiscal burden. Therefore, a limiting factor was introduced, i.e., households living in accommodations above average rents had to bear a higher fraction of housing costs themselves.

Sweden has pioneered with an interesting innovation. The government pays the highest percentage of the gap for the more expensive dwelling units rather than for the less expensive. For example, in 1973, a family with two children and a net annual income of $2,229 (SK 10,000) received a government subsidy of around $27 per month (SK 120) if it obtained an apartment at $92 (SK 400) a month; the government's share of the rent was about 30 percent. If the family obtained an apartment at $137 (SK 600), the government subsidy and share were around $55 (SK 240) and 40 percent, respectively. At a rent of around $166 (SK 725), the subsidy and the percentage were at a maximum, i.e., at $70 (SK 310) and 42.74 percent. At rents beyond this level, the percentage declined. The rationale was twofold. First, new construction costs in 1972-74 rose so high that the government could not find renters for a large number of recently built social housing. Second, the government had a specific objective of increasing the quality of housing of its citizens, particularly in regard to living space. Therefore, special financial incentives were created to encourage movement of families to larger apartments.

Summary

The first central issue in defining a reasonable housing allowance is: What rent can a family afford to pay? Governments have promulgated a wide range of shelter-to-income ratios that households can be expected to pay, varying from zero for very low-income families in some countries, such as the United Kingdom, to a maximum of 30 percent. The average appears to be between 10 and 15 percent. A key factor is the number of children; in most countries the maximum percentage of income paid for rent declines as the number of children increases.

The second element is: What is a reasonable household income ceiling for housing allowance participants? A few governments established simple, formal income ceilings, such as the 75th percentile of income in the Netherlands. Most countries, however, adopted more complicated methods, taking into account family size, size of dwelling, size of urban area, and rent ceilings. In many plans the income ceiling appears to reflect the poverty or subsistence level.

The third major issue in the design of a housing allowance system is the establishment of a rent ceiling. In most countries the ceiling aims to cover the costs of minimum-standard housing. The most widely used guide is probably the average rent in the housing market area. Some plans also adopted the concept of a minimum rent, the rationale being that all persons have a moral obligation to make some kind of payment toward household rent.

The final question is: How much of the gap between actual rents for decent housing and the rents that families can afford to pay should be covered by government subsidy? Many governments pay 100 percent of the gap to avoid sacrificing vital elements in the family's level of living. A majority, however, cover only part of the gap, ranging from 50 to 90 percent, mainly for two reasons: (1) to avoid the heavy tax burden involved in 100 percent coverage; and (2) to provide an incentive for households not to select the most expensive rents offered in the market.

NOTES

1. International Labour Office, *Workers' Housing* (Geneva: International Labour Office, 1959), 9-11.
2. International Labour Office, *Household Income and Expenditure Statistics, 1968-1976* (Geneva: International Labour Office, 1979), 289-92.
3. International Labour Office, *Workers' Housing, op. cit.,* 9-11.
4. Australia, Ministry for Works and Housing, *Homes for Australia* (Canberra: Ministry for Works and Housing, 1949), 5.
5. Michael Dennis and Susan Fish, *Programs in Search of a Policy* (Toronto: Hakkert, 1972), 58-59; Albert Rose, *Canadian Housing Policies: 1935–1980* (Toronto: Butterworths, 1980), 9.
6. Paul Burke, Connie Casey, and Gerd Doepner, *Housing Affordability Problems and Housing Need in Canada and the United States: A Comparative Study* (Washington, D.C.: U.S. Department of Housing and Urban Development, 1981), 8.
7. New Zealand, National Housing Commission, *Housing New Zealand* (Wellington: National Housing Commission, 1978), 67-68.
8. Terry S. Lane, *What Families Spend for Housing: The Origins and Uses of the "Rules of Thumb"* (Washington, D.C.: U.S. Department of Housing and Urban Development, 1977), Chap. 1; *see also* Judith D. Feins and Charles S. White, Jr., *The Ratio of Shelter Expenditures to Income: Definitional Issues, Typical Patterns, and Historical Trends* (Cambridge, MA: Abt Associates, 1977), Chaps. I and II.
9. E. Jay Howenstine, *Attacking Housing Costs* (Rutgers University: Center for Urban Policy Research, New Brunswick, NJ, 1983), Chap. 1.
10. Hugo Priemus, *Housing Allowances in the Netherlands* (Delft: Delft University Press, 1984), 10-12.
11. Jacques Badet (Chairman), *Report of the Working Group on the Reform of Personal Housing Assistance* (Germantown, MD: HUD USER, 1984), 124. Translation of *Rapport Du Groupe De Travail Sur La Reforme Des Aides Personnelles Au Logement* (Paris: Ministry of Urban Planning and Housing, 1982).
12. N. Zeyl, "Systems of Individual Subsidies" in United Nations Economic Commission for Europe, Committee on Housing, Building and Planning, *Financing of Housing* (Geneva: U.N. Economic Commission for Europe, 1973), 156, 168-72.
13. Eugen Dick, *Distribution of Housing Costs Between the Public Sector and Individuals* (Geneva: United Nations, 1977), 22. Discussion paper prepared for the

Seminar on Housing Policy convened by the United Nations Economic Commission for Europe, Committee on Housing, Building and Planning.

14. Michael John Oxley, "Housing Policy in Western Europe: An Economic Analysis of the Aims and Instruments of Housing Policy in the United Kingdom, West Germany, France, the Netherlands, Denmark, and Ireland" (Ph.D. diss., Leicester University, 1983), 294-95.

15. Federal Republic of Germany, Bundesministerium fur Raumordnung, Bauwesen und Stadtebau, *Housing Allowance and Rent: 1983 Report* (Germantown, MD: HUD USER, 1984), 9. Translation of *Wohngeld und Mietenbericht 1983* (Bonn, 1984).

16. Keijo Tanner, *The Finnish Housing Allowance System for Families and Single Persons as Applied in 1983* (Helsinki: National Housing Board, 1983), 2-3 and App. 3.

17. For a discussion of the five demands on the Swedish means test—that the test is done on relevant grounds, that it is carried out in a fair manner, that it is based on the household's current conditions, that the information is easy to find, and that the test does not infringe on the applicant's integrity—*see* Sweden, Housing Subsidy Committee, *Housing Subsidies* (Germantown, MD: HUD USER, 1982), 6-9. Translation of *Bostads Bidragen* (Stockholm: Ministry of Housing and Physical Planning, 1982).

18. J. Barry Cullingworth, *Housing Allowances: The British Experience* (Toronto: Centre for Community Studies, University of Toronto, 1977), 18-19.

19. Hugo Priemus, *op. cit.*, 70-71.

20. J. Barry Cullingworth, *op. cit.*, 21.

21. Canada, Task Force on Shelter and Incomes, *Report 1* (Ottawa: Central Mortgage and Housing Corporation, 1976), 58-59, 63.

22. Keijo Tanner, *op. cit.*, App. 1.

23. Australia, Department of Works and Housing, *Housing* (Sydney: Scotow Press, 1946), 7-8.

24. K. F. Watson, F. Ermuth, and W. Hamilton, *A Comparative Analysis of Housing Allowance Programs* (Ottawa: Central Mortgage and Housing Corporation, 1978), E6.

4

Qualifying Conditions
for the Housing Allowance

Having defined the elements of a reasonable housing allowance system from the individual's point of view, it is now appropriate to examine issues which must be settled before the housing allowance becomes an operational system.

Physical Structure

In European countries the building code system has been the traditional means of promoting and maintaining minimum-housing standards. Since the early part of the century, if not before, all new private and public construction has had to meet building code requirements. Landlords were informed of code violations, and compliance generally has been good. Consequently, most of the European housing stock is well constructed, although some lacks certain modern plumbing facilities and may not have been adequately maintained.

As long as housing assistance was in the form of producer subsidies, no great problem arose regarding the quality of new housing construction. Almost by definition, public housing was built according to at least contemporary minimum standards; governments did not deliberately set out to build new slums. But when in the post-World War II period the consumer housing subsidy began to grow in prominence, the issue of minimum-housing standards arose.

If, in an effort to relieve an excessive rent burden, a housing allowance were paid to a family living in substandard or slum conditions, this would be in conflict with the basic objective of a public housing subsidy policy to provide decent housing for all families. The problem was, therefore, to design a housing allowance system that would either: (1) bring substandard accommodations up to minimum standards; or (2) bring about the replacement of the substandard housing, if it were neither technically nor economically practicable to upgrade it.

The first obvious step in eradicating substandard housing, therefore, was to require that the physical structure meet minimum housing standards. Most countries made that a condition of their housing allowance systems, although this has been carried out in different ways with varying degrees of rigor.

Some housing allowance systems, including those of Austria, France, Denmark, Norway, Sweden, and Zurich (Switzerland), require that the floor area or number of rooms be commensurate with the size of the family, and that the dwelling must not exceed a specified maximum area nor be less than a specified minimum area. In the initial Swedish system, for example, the rule was that the minimum size house should have no more than two persons per room, with the kitchen not counting as a room. Other systems, such as Tyrol and Vorarlberg provinces (Austria) and Basle Canton (Switzerland), only have a general proscription that the dwelling must be of an adequate size, or, as in Finland, "proper for living" or, as in the case of the Federal Republic of Germany, "suitable as a place of abode."

Fairly detailed building code regulations are to be found in most European countries. France has a stringent set of rules regarding minimum housing standards and amenities. Depending on the size of the family, there must be a minimum number of rooms (e.g., three rooms for a household of four persons); the amenities must include a drinking water tap, a device for evacuating used water, a means of heating, and a toilet in the dwelling or in the case of apartment buildings on the floor or landing; and floor areas, height of rooms, and size of windows must meet specified standards. Denmark and Canada (the rent supplement program) require certification that the dwellings of housing allowance recipients meet certain standards of quality. The New Brunswick provincial system (Canada) requires that the dwelling unit be self-contained, and that it be inspected for conformity with health and safety regulations.

In the United States Experimental Housing Allowance Program (EHAP), one-half of those enrolled in the supply experiment lived in dwellings that did not meet minimum standards. Two-thirds of these repaired their houses at an average cost of about $100 in order to qualify, while one-third dropped out. The supply experiment therefore increased the likelihood of occupying standard housing from about 50 percent to 80 percent.[1] On the other hand, the minimum housing standard requirements were a major deterrent to participation in the demand experiment. Participation rates in those sites requiring minimum housing standards were around 45 percent, only about one-half the participation rates at those sites in the demand experiment which made no such requirements.[2]

It should be pointed out that in the demand experiment two types of housing requirements were used: minimum standards and minimum rent. Under the minimum-housing standard requirements, only participants occupying dwellings that met certain physical and occupancy standards received an allowance. If participants occupied units that did not meet these standards, they either had to move or bring their units up to the standards. Participants already living in standard housing could use their allowance to pay for better housing or reduce their rent burden.

Minimum rent—the second approach in the demand experiment—was considered as a relatively inexpensive and reasonably accurate alternative to minimum standards in order to observe differences in response and cost. The test assumed, first, that housing quality could be broadly defined to include all residential services, and second, that rent levels were highly correlated with the level of residential services.[3] The requirement that recipients spend a minimum amount on rent did not prove to be a good proxy for minimum physical standards.[4]

There are two additional special conditions which some foreign governments incorporated in their housing allowance systems, the intent—or at least the effect—of which is indirectly to help ensure that participants live in minimum-standard housing. The first is to limit the system to families living in housing financed or owned by public authorities. The assumption is that since public authorities would not consider financing substandard housing, any structures financed by producer housing subsidies would, by definition, be acceptable housing. Thus, in Austria housing allowances are limited to publicly financed buildings, while in the Netherlands, prior to 1975 (now all low-income renters qualify) renters automatically qualified when they lived in developments where major improvements had been carried out with state assistance. In both Norway and the United Kingdom housing allowances are restricted to households living in public housing or in rent-controlled developments in the private sector.

The second condition relates to the construction date. One of the main objectives in many housing allowance systems has been to stimulate demand for recent postwar housing, which consists of high-quality structures and incorporates modern amenities, but which—because of its high cost and rent levels—might otherwise remain idle on account of insufficient demand. This condition is examined later in the section "Construction Date" of this chapter.

On the other hand, it should be pointed out that some countries have not made minimum standards a condition for receiving the allowance. The Federal Republic of Germany, Finland, the Netherlands, Sweden, and the United Kingdom pay a housing allowance to qualifying low-income families without inquiring into the quality of their accommodation. In the early 1970s, Sweden abolished all requirements relating to the size and equipment of the dwelling; in Finland, this happened in 1975. Similarly in the proposed Australian housing allowance system, no account was taken of the condition of the housing accommodation. Most provincial shelter allowance programs in Canada do not require inspection of dwelling units.

Several considerations help to explain the apparent lack of concern in some countries for housing quality. First of all, inspecting the dwelling of each applicant and monitoring its condition through the years are costly administrative burdens. Second, in most cases, such inspection would be regarded as unnecessary because of the already generally good quality of the existing housing stock. This is especially true of Australia and Sweden.

Third, if the housing allowance is tied to housing standard requirements, this may have unintended negative effects. A family may be certified to receive a housing allowance, but it may not be able to find housing of acceptable quality within the maximum allowable rent under the program. If, then, the family seeks housing above the rent ceiling and pays the extra amount out of its own income, then it may end up with as excessive a rent burden as before. A housing allowance may not, therefore, be an altogether satisfactory approach to the problem of substandard housing if acceptable vacant accommodations are in short supply.[5]

The negative effect of tying housing allowances to minimum housing standards appears to be confirmed in a study of American experience prepared for the Canada Mortgage and Housing Corporation. The authors conclude:

"In our opinion, untied transfers are clearly preferable: when payments are tied to minimum standards tests for housing, the effect is to reduce participation among groups one would most like to serve, and to foster relatively inefficient (and perhaps counter-productive) housing search behavior among the remainder."[6]

Finally, some maintain that the basic objective of the housing allowance system is to overcome the excessive rent burden on low-income household budgets, and not necessarily to bring living conditions up to minimum standard levels. Even though a dwelling unit may fail to meet certain minor requirements, its habitability may, nevertheless, be generally good.

An important trend in some housing allowance systems is to promote housing consumption above minimum physical standards. As observed in Chapter 3 (Unaffordable Gap to Be Covered by Subsidy), Swedish policy provides a financial incentive for families to raise housing quality well above minimum standards. The size of the housing allowance increases, both relatively and absolutely, when the family rents the more expensive (within rather wide limits), rather than the less expensive, unit. This policy has also been followed to some degree in other countries, such as Denmark, France, Norway, and the Netherlands.

Eligible Households

Foreign governments approached housing allowances with caution. Practically all had large, well-established producer housing subsidies as the central thrust in their slum clearance programs. Initially the consumer subsidy approach was viewed as a supplement, not a substitute, for producer housing subsidies. It was designed primarily to meet special hardship situations not being met by the producer subsidy program. It was only after some experience that governments began to think that the housing allowance might become the main, or at least one of the main, pillars of the housing finance system. Accordingly, the scope of eligible households gradually evolved and broadened.

In the early days of the housing allowance, as observed in Chapter 2, the large family was regarded as the neediest group in the population. Housing requirements weigh heavily on the large family's budget in two respects: (1) the larger the family, the greater the shelter space required; and (2) the larger the family, the greater the living costs of food and clothing, leaving little for housing accommodation. It is not surprising, then, that in most systems children quickly became a criterion of eligibility.

In the early Danish and Swedish systems, only families with at least one child qualified for the housing allowance. Two or more children were required for family eligibility in France. In the Swiss Canton of Basle and the city of Zurich, only large families qualified (i.e., presumably more than two children).

Conversely, in a further reinforcement of the large family ethos, some countries specifically excluded households without children. France declared two categories ineligible: (1) actively employed, married couples, who have been married for five years and are without dependents; and (2) single persons between the ages of 25 and 65. Similarly, Norway's housing allowance system excluded actively employed, childless couples and most persons living alone. In Denmark most persons living alone have been ineligible for housing allowances. The Finnish system excludes couples who have been married over 30 years, "all-adult households," and unmarried couples living together. The assumption underlying such restrictions is that, being spared the financial burden of raising children, these households should take care of themselves without state assistance.

A second category of the population recognized as an area of special need early in the development of the housing allowance was the elderly. The principal reason for the weak economic status of elderly persons is, of course, the fact that by and large they cease to receive regular earned income. While most European countries have long had old-age pension systems and the coverage has been comparatively wide, pensions have, for the most part, been extremely modest. It was, therefore, a logical development that housing allowances should be introduced as a supplementary form of assistance, particularly to meet increases in shelter cost, as rent controls were relaxed.

Another category—relatively much smaller but nevertheless possessing intrinsic public appeal—frequently combined with the elderly in various social measures is the physically handicapped.

As time passed, the strong supply pressure for producer housing systems declined, and the practicability of consumer housing subsidies was confirmed in experience. Gradually, eligibility requirements for consumer housing subsidies became less restrictive and were increasingly open to all households carrying an excessive rent burden. Today, a number of countries, including Austria, the Federal Republic of Germany, the Netherlands (only renters), the United Kingdom, and the United States, define eligibility broadly to include almost all low-income households.[7]

Tenure Qualifications

Historically, European urban, low-income families lived almost entirely in rental housing—public or private. As a whole, they had neither the expectation nor—much more important—the financial means to acquire ownership. Housing allowance systems, therefore, have been designed mainly for low-income renters.

Some systems, such as the early French rent subsidy for the needy aged and disabled, specifically excluded homeowners. Some systems, such as the Swiss Canton of Basle and the city of Zurich, virtually excluded homeowners as potential beneficiaries. Still other countries, such as Australia, Canada (provinces), Denmark, the Netherlands, and the United Kingdom, designed their systems for renters only.

The exclusion of homeowners has been based on three major considerations. First, it was believed that anyone who had enough capital to buy a house was almost by definition not classifiable as needy. Second, in many countries homeowners already received subsidies, e.g., in the form of preferential interest rates and tax deductability of mortgage interest payments and insurance payments. In Ireland and the United Kingdom, it has been customary for mortgagors to take out life insurance as a protection for the mortgagee. In the Netherlands, a special premium is paid to new homeowners. Third, prices in the owner-occupied sector are uncontrolled.

On the other hand, some governments, including Austria, Finland, France, the Federal Republic of Germany, Norway, Sweden, and the United States, opened housing allowance systems to both renters and homeowners. The rationale for including homeowners is that all low-income families deserve equal treatment irrespective of differences in regard to their capital holdings. Thus the justification for extending coverage of the proposed Quebec provincial (Canada) housing allowance plan to low-income, senior citizen homeowners was that, although they might be property rich, they were income poor. Quebec property values had not been inflated as much as in other parts of Canada, and it seemed socially undesirable to force pensioners to sell their homes in order to qualify for a housing allowance.[8]

It is not to be overlooked, too, that, as a tenure, home ownership promotes other desirable social virtues, such as greater efforts to maintain and improve the housing stock, neighborhood pride, and greater social stability. Although home ownership is often subsidized in principle, in practice low-income wage earners may benefit little, if any, from the deductibility of mortgage interest payments from income tax, since in many countries they pay little, if any, income tax.

The inclusion of home ownership in housing allowance plans has, however, generally been circumscribed. For example, the 1976 Austrian amendment extending the housing allowance to homeowners limited it to "young families and families with three or more children" with monthly incomes of less than $867 (AS12,600; 1978) and provided that mortgage payments (covering interest at 1/2 of 1 percent and amortization of principal) plus an amount to ensure proper maintenance of the dwelling did not exceed 5 percent of the family income.[9] The Finnish housing allowance system includes only owners of dwellings which were constructed in 1974 or later or which were renovated in 1981 or later.[10]

Finally, it is worthwhile noting the position of subtenants in housing allowance systems. In the Zurich housing allowance system, subletting leads to disqualification. In Finland, the Netherlands, and the Tyrolean provincial system (Austria), payment of housing allowances to subtenants is expressly prohibited.

Construction Date

Date of construction has, surprisingly enough, been a condition for the payment of housing allowances in many countries. Its importance derives from its role in determining cost and rent levels.

Before World War II, building costs were relatively stable over long periods of time. Since World War II, however, inflationary rates of increase in housing costs have been typical in most industrialized countries. As a result, housing costs in one decade—and the rents based on them—may be well above those of the previous decade.

These cost and rent differentials have been magnified by the continuation of wartime rent controls into the postwar period. Long-standing tenants, often in the inner city occupying large dwelling units, had little incentive to give up low-rent accommodations even though their housing requirements were shrinking as children grew up and left home. On the other hand, the housing available to recent entrants into the housing market, such as young families and families moving to expanding industries and regions, was largely confined to more recent construction built at high housing costs and carrying high rents. As a matter of fact in several countries, including Denmark, the Federal Republic of Germany, the Netherlands, Sweden, and Switzerland, the supply of recently completed vacant dwellings grew to alarming levels, particularly in 1973-74.

Concern for minimum housing standards appears to have been another important consideration leading governments to deny housing allowances to households living in old dwelling units. While masonry buildings of 100 years or more (common in European cities) might be structurally sound, their sanitary and heating equipment were often either nonexistent or quite deficient. It was, therefore, not unusual for prewar housing to be ineligible for housing allowances.

In Sweden, under the family housing allowance system established in 1947, a dwelling must have been erected or converted after December 31, 1947, in order to qualify, while under the pensioner's housing allowance system adopted in 1958, the effective date was July 1, 1946. These restrictions have now been abolished. The cutoff date for the age of dwelling units in the Dutch housing allowance system (before 1975) was 1960, and in the Norwegian housing allowance system, 1962.

Residence Requirements

As a rule, a household must have a permanent residence in order to qualify for a housing allowance. There are, however, various interpretations of what constitutes a permanent resident. For example, a student who lives in an apartment separate from his parents may qualify for a housing allowance in Denmark, but not in the Federal Republic of Germany.

The issue becomes more sticky in the case of provincial plans within a country, where persons might gravitate to a province solely to obtain a housing allowance—and thereby be an extra burden on the taxpayers of that province. In Canada, the British Columbia system for senior citizens requires two years of residence immediately prior to application or a continuous five-year period at any one time. In the Austrian province of Vorarlberg and in the Swiss Canton of Basle, only citizens of the country are eligible. The Zurich (Switzerland) municipal housing allowance system is limited to citizens of the municipality. In some cases, however, such residence requirements are relaxed if the foreigner has resided a minimum period in the canton, or if there is a reciprocity agreement between the claimant's country and the country of residence.

Summary

Housing allowance systems vary considerably in the conditions which they require of participants. The most important is that the physical structure must meet minimum housing standards, although not all governments have this requirement.

In the early development of housing systems, eligibility tended to be narrowly defined so as to include only certain hardship categories, such as large families and the elderly. As governments acquired more experience with the consumer-type subsidy, the scope gradually enlarged so that now most low-income households are included in most systems.

Governments are about evenly divided with regard to the inclusion of low-income homeowners.

NOTES

1. Ira S. Lowry, *Experimenting With Housing Allowances* (Santa Monica: Rand Corporation, 1982), vi.
2. Stephen D. Kennedy and Jean MacMillan, *Participation Under Alternative Housing Allowance Programs: Evidence From the Housing Allowance Demand Experiment* (Cambridge, MA: Abt Associates, 1980), S-3.
3. *Ibid.*, A-6-7.
4. Joseph Friedman and Daniel H. Weinberg, *Housing Consumption Under a Constrained Income Transfer: Evidence From a Housing Gap Housing Allowance* (Cambridge, MA: Abt Associates, 1980), 56.
5. Association of Municipalities of Ontario, *Shelter Allowances* (Toronto: Association of Municipalities of Toronto, 1980), 8.

6. Peter H. Rossi, Andy B. Anderson, and James D. Wright, *Housing Consumption Effects of Guaranteed Annual Income Experiments* (Ottawa: Canada Mortgage and Housing Corporation, 1982), 105.

7. For an interesting discussion of technical eligibility criteria, *see* Canada, Task Force on Shelter and Incomes, *Report 1* (Ottawa: Central Mortgage and Housing Corporation, 1976), 69-70.

8. Janet McClain, ed., *Are Housing Allowances the Answer?* (Ottawa: Canadian Council on Social Development, 1979), 29.

9. Austria, Ministry of Construction and Technology, *Trends and Policies in the Field of Housing, Building and Planning* (Vienna: Ministry of Construction and Technology, 1978), 4-5.

10. Keijo Tanner, *The Finnish Housing Allowance System for Families and Single Persons as Applied in 1983* (Helsinki: National Housing Board, 1983), 3.

5

Administrative Arrangements

There are a number of issues in the effective administration of housing allowance systems: enrollment; annual recertification; forms and frequency of payment; support services; division of administrative and financial responsibility; and administrative costs. This chapter undertakes a comparative review of foreign experience on these issues.[1]

Enrollment

To an outsider it may not appear that enrollment in a housing allowance system would pose a problem. If, as a national policy, it is decided that to make decent housing affordable, needy persons have a right to a housing allowance, then it might be presumed that all needy people would be delighted to receive such an allowance and that such a system could be automatically instituted. This is far from the case.

In the first place, no government has readily available, complete data on who are the needy households. The eligibility of a household can only be determined after it has been checked against the prescribed conditions for participation. This may be a long and complex process.

Second, many households do not apply for a housing allowance, even though it is their right. Nevertheless, foreign housing allowance systems achieved considerably higher participation rates than the approximately 33 percent of eligible renters achieved in the United States EHAP supply experiments and the approximately 50 percent achieved in the demand experiments. In 1979 the United Kingdom Department of the Environment estimated the take-up for rent rebates in the public sector in England and Wales to be 72 percent; for rent allowances in the private sector, it was 50 percent.[2] The estimated take-up in the Federal Republic of Germany has been around 75 percent[3] and in the Netherlands around 75 percent,[4] while in the British Columbia (Canada) housing allowance program, it has been approximately 60 percent.[5]

The reasons for these disappointing enrollment rates are many. Pride has often prevented a family from accepting what may be regarded as charity. Furthermore, it may be demeaning to go through the means test in order to qualify. Many families found bureaucratic procedures involved in eligibility determination forbidding and something to be avoided at all costs. In some cases, tenants of private dwellings have been reluctant to claim allowances for fear of landlord disapproval.[6] Minimum housing standards may prove a deterrent for some families; they may prefer to live in substandard housing in familiar surroundings rather than undergo a move to a minimum-standard dwelling in a new community in order to obtain the housing allowance. In other cases, the amount of the allowance may be so small that the family does not find it worthwhile. Still other families are so disinterested in life that they remain forever ignorant of options. One of the major factors explaining the participation rate in Canada was that the poorest families tended to be the least educated and least capable of reading brochures and filling out complicated application forms.[7] The city of Birmingham, United Kingdom, one of the most innovative urban areas in housing allowances, similarly found it particularly difficult to obtain enrollment of the elderly. It was necessary to make arrangements to give them every help and, in most cases, to have somebody fill in the forms for them.[8]

In the U.S. EHAP supply experiment the main reasons for nonparticipation were the small entitlements and the unwillingness of some households living in substandard dwellings to either repair them or move to better housing.[9] In the EHAP demand experiment the reasons most often given for refusing participation were program requirements (such as monthly income reports and periodic housing evaluations) and reluctance to accept money from the government.[10]

Persuading needy households that it is in their interest to participate in housing allowance systems, therefore, is a major task in program administration. Governments have approached this problem in different ways with varying degrees of success.

One way of promoting a higher enrollment rate has been a national publicity campaign. In the 1970s the Dutch government launched an extensive advertising campaign for its housing allowance program through newspapers and television.

In the United Kingdom, the response to the 1972 housing allowance system was very slow. By November, 1973, only 8 percent of the tenants in the private sector as compared to 75 percent of the tenants in the public housing sector had enrolled. Consequently, the Department of the Environment spent approximately $2 million on publicizing the housing allowance program from September, 1972, to April, 1975. The effort consisted mainly of annually placing two major advertisements in all newspapers and making pamphlets available locally. By April, 1975, the private sector participation rate had risen to 25 percent. Gradually, thereafter, the responsibility for program publicity was shifted from the central government to local authorities.

In the winter of 1974-75, another British effort was made through two pilot campaigns launched in Bristol and Westminster to raise the level of participation still higher. Trained canvassers visited potential claimants of welfare benefits in order to assess their eligibility, and when appropriate, to encourage application. This was regarded as the best means for overcoming widespread reluctance to apply for means-tested benefits. Two canvassing methods were adopted. In Bristol, where fewer difficulties were anticipated, it was decided to canvas large areas having readily accessible tenants, to limit callbacks to one, and to drop publicity leaflets where no personal contact was made. Canvassers were not expected to enter into detailed counseling, but instead referred tenants to full-time rent allowance officers who were prepared to visit potential participants as part of their everyday duties. In Westminster, where earlier studies had found tenants difficult to contact, a more intensive campaign was mounted and concentrated in four small areas. Canvassers were expected to make as many callbacks as necessary and to engage in detailed counseling in order to assess eligibility accurately and to encourage applications.

Canvass results were disappointing. In Bristol, the total take-up of eligible households was raised from between 17.4 and 19.7 percent to between 20.4 and 23.1 percent. In Westminster, the take-up in the four areas was increased from 15 to 32 percent, but in the city as a whole the increase was only marginal. The canvassing approach encountered three main obstacles. Tenants proved difficult to contact, and only a small proportion appeared eligible despite careful selection of the canvassing area. Accurate assessment of entitlement was rarely possible, partly because tenants gave inadequate information and partly because the canvassers failed to understand fully the housing allowance system. Finally, many eligible tenants were resistant to the idea of applying for a means-tested housing allowance. While canvassing obtained small increases in enrollments, it placed a considerable burden on local authorities and was believed impractical as a general solution to the low take-up of housing allowances.[11] It may be observed incidentally that the proposed Australian housing allowance experiment also planned to have counselors work at the neighborhood level to contact difficult-to-reach families.

Sweden used the income tax system to stimulate enrollment in its housing allowance program. Income tax returns were screened by computer to identify households whose size and income seemed to indicate they would be eligible for a housing allowance. An application form and enrollment instructions were then sent to each identified family. This approach seems to have been relatively successful in reaching families. In 1976, 650,000 households with children, or 50 percent of the total, and 700,000 one-adult households, or 90 percent of the total, were enrolled.

Annual Recertification

One of the heavy burdens on housing allowance administration is to monitor the continued eligibility of participants. Although many conditions, such as dwelling unit quality and the number of family members, need checking out, the chief problem is to adjust allowances to changes in household income.

The general practice is to reexamine the income status of participants once a year, placing the responsibility on recipients to report notable changes in income in the course of the year. Governments, such as Sweden, which have linked housing allowance systems to income tax machinery, have a relatively efficient, built-in method of adjusting housing allowances to family income changes. In systems without a systematic hookup with the income tax system, monitoring the income position of housing allowance recipients can become a laborious administrative process.

One of the problems encountered arises from the failure of national legislatures to provide for frequent adjustment of allowance ceilings to take account of increases in income attributable to general inflation. Although such increases in income may appear to be an improvement in financial positions, the real poverty situation may have remained unchanged. As a result families have been penalized unfairly by being cut off from the system.

Form and Frequency of Payment

Normally the housing allowance is paid to the occupant by some government body. In many systems, however, the allowance may be paid to either the tenant or the owner, e.g., in Denmark, Finland, France, the

Federal Republic of Germany, the Netherlands, Norway, Sweden, Switzerland, and the United Kingdom.

There has been considerable discussion about who should receive the payment: the tenant or the landlord. A strong case is made for the tenant being the direct beneficiary; in fact, the central concept in the consumer subsidy approach is that the subsidy should be attached to the consumer, not to the producer. Moreover, the allowance should be portable, that is, it should go with the consumer wherever the household should live. Since the head of the household carries the excessive rent burden, there is psychological value in that person receiving the subsidy that reduces the burden to a fair level. It preserves self-respect and tends to enhance the bargaining position of the renter vis-à-vis the landlord in attempting to maintain a high level of housing services.

On the other hand, if the tenant receives the allowance, then there is the risk that the person may spend the "rent money" on other consumption and as a result fall in rent arrears. To eliminate the risk of an improvident tenant misusing the housing allowance, some systems provide the option of payment to the landlord, the mortgagee, or the guarantor.

Payment to the landlord has, however, certain disadvantages. It strengthens his position vis-à-vis the tenant in disputes about the level of housing services, thus perhaps tending toward a lower level of expenditures on maintenance and repair than might otherwise be the case. Direct receipt of the allowance might also encourage the landlord to raise rents more than would otherwise be the case.

In the case of tenants living in municipally owned housing, the usual practice is for the payment to go directly from the central government to the local authority. This is efficient from the administrative point of view.

As regards frequency of payment, the usual practice is for the allowance to be paid monthly in arrears. However, in the United Kingdom, it is paid weekly following the local practice of weekly rent collection. In Austria and the Federal Republic of Germany, it may be paid on either a monthly or quarterly basis. In some Swiss cantons, payment is made on a quarterly or semiannual basis, depending on the amount. It should be noted, too, that the Federal Republic of Germany pays the allowance in advance, making it easier for the tenant to pay rent in advance.

Support Services

Various kinds of services have been offered by governments directly or indirectly in connection with housing allowance systems. In the United Kingdom, counseling and market information are provided separately through Housing Aid Centres in many metro areas, and through the social welfare programs for which many of those eligible for allowances are qualified. In the Netherlands, removal grants are paid to some tenants if they are vacating a dwelling that is substandard or that is a large prewar house with a low rent, and if they are moving to a higher rent dwelling, possibly with much smaller space.

In the United States, EHAP experience demonstrated that local responsive support services, for example, legal assistance to ensure equal opportunity for minority groups such as blacks, or availability of transportation and/or child care services to facilitate attendance of participants at counseling sessions, were an especially important factor in successful implementation of a housing allowance system in a tight market.[12]

In 1966 Belgium introduced several incentives for families to relocate from substandard housing to satisfactory habitation. They included a resettlement allowance of $40 (BF2,000), an installation allowance of $40 (BF2,000), and a three-year monthly rent allowance not to exceed $16 (BF800) to help cover the gap between the rent on the old unit and the rent on the new unit.[13]

Support services tend to enhance the effectiveness of a housing allowance system. When they are provided directly by the housing allowance program, however, they inescapably add to the administrative costs of the program.

Coordination and Integration of Housing Allowance Systems

Many countries, including Australia, Denmark, Finland, France, Norway, Sweden, and the United Kingdom, have more than one housing allowance system. The degree to which governments have achieved coordination among the different systems varies considerably.

For example, the Swedish Housing Subsidy Committee has focused on the administrative complexities of the national housing allowance system and the local housing supplement system.[14] In the mid-1970s there were almost no similarities between the two systems because they served different groups, they were developed independently of each other, and they were administered by different agencies. Since then significant steps have been taken to obtain a more equitable treatment for recipients in the two systems in regard to such elements as income tests, rent ceilings, methods of calculating housing costs, percentage of gap coverage, and considerations for children.

Similarly, in France, the existence of three different housing allowance systems—the Family Housing Allowance, the Social Housing Allowance, and the Personalized Housing Allowance—and the higher priority given to home ownership have led to widespread criticism of "the lack of equity among households."[15] In 1981 the French National Assembly adopted a two-year plan aiming to effect a gradual consolidation of the three housing allowance systems. In 1982 a notable Working Group on the Reform of Personal Housing Assistance recommended a single housing allowance system to replace the three separate systems based on the principle "that all tenants are ultimately entitled to benefit from the new personal assistance"[16] and proposed a transition plan to implement this objective.

Administrative Costs

Administrative costs are difficult to compare from country to country. Costs allocated to the housing allowance system in some countries may be covered differently in other countries. In Austria, for example, provincial governments provide administrative services for the national system, which is financed by the federal budget. Data on average administrative costs per family may reflect a simple proportion of total housing payments or an estimate of the marginal cost of administering the housing allowance program as one program among many. There is also considerable variation in the functions which various housing allowance administrations carry out in applying the law, e.g., certification and recertification of dwelling unit fitness, enrollment outreach, and participant services. Moreover, cost data that are available do not relate to the same year. Therefore, cost comparisons can only be of limited value.

Administrative costs appear to be lowest in the Scandinavian countries and in the Federal Republic of Germany. They were estimated to be about 2.5 percent in Finland in 1983,[17] 3 percent in Denmark, 5 percent in Sweden, and 8.6 percent in the Federal Republic of Germany.[18] In the United Kingdom, the Department of Environment reported administrative costs of around 17 percent, while in France they have been estimated to range between 12 and 15 percent. In the United Kingdom, the cost of administering private rent allowances has been almost double the cost of rent rebates on public housing.[19]

By comparison, in the United States Experimental Housing Allowance Program annual housing allowance payments averaged $969 in the Administrative Agency Experiment, while administrative costs per family averaged $276, or approximately 22 percent of total costs. In both the United Kingdom and the United States, outreach enrollment efforts proved very costly. In one London borough the cost of an experimental campaign to enroll tenants in the private rental sector ranged from around $5 to $30 (£7 to £43), or an average of $15 (£32) per successful applicant. Inspections and income certification also pushed costs up very much in the United States.

Summary

One of the most difficult administrative problems has been to enroll all those entitled to receive a housing allowance. No country has succeeded in enrolling more than 90 percent of the eligible households. Many factors contribute to the shortfall—pride, ignorance, smallness of allowance, the hassle of the means test, and bureaucratic procedures.

Recertification of eligibility is generally done on an annual basis. Normally the allowance is paid to the occupant, but some plans provide for payment to the owner as well.

Quite aside from bureaucratic obstacles, one of the major deterrents to the consolidation of two or more plans into a single, comprehensive national system is the question of higher costs. In simplifying and streamlining housing allowances, the tendency is to select the most generous treatment that has been applied on each major issue in the separate systems and to generalize it throughout the new unified system. The pressures to convert the housing allowance into a universal entitlement on a liberal basis become formidable.

NOTES

1. For a good review of administrative issues and recommendations thereon, *see* Charles Legg and Marion Brion, *The Administration of the Rent Rebate and Rent Allowance Schemes* (London: Department of the Environment, 1976). *See also* John Trutko, Otto J. Hetzel, and A. David Yates, *A Comparison of the Experimental Housing Allowance Program and Great Britian's Rent Allowance Program* (Washington, D.C.: Urban Institute, 1978).

2. Michael John Oxley, "Housing Policy in Western Europe: An Economic Analysis of the Aims and Instruments of Housing Policy in the United Kingdom, West Germany, France, the Netherlands, Denmark and Ireland" (Ph.D. diss., Leicester University, England 1983) 293.

3. K. F. Watson, F. Ermuth, and W. Hamilton, *A Comparative Analysis of Allowance Programs* (Ottawa: Central Mortgage and Housing Corporation, 1978), E12.

4. In 1983, the take-up rate declined, perhaps temporarily, to 70 percent. Hugo Priemus, *Housing Allowances in the Netherlands* (Delft: Delft University Press, 1984), 60. A study in 1981 showed that there were 750,000 eligible renters entitled to an average allowance of $499 (FL1,246) or a total of $375 million (FL935 million), although actually there were only 528,782 recipients at an average allowance of $637 (FL1,589) or a total of $337 million (FL841 million). There was therefore a latent demand of 29 percent in terms of participation and 10 percent in terms of budget. *Ibid.*, 55. *See also* W. Wiewel, *Housing Allowances and the Dutch Rent Subsidy Program* (Santa Monica: Rand Corporation, 1979), 4, 8.

5. *See* Marion Steele's (University of Guelph) unpublished study on housing allowances for the Ontario Economic Council in 1982, Chap. 5.

6. Malcolm Wicks, "Helping the Rent Payer," *Housing Review* (September-October 1974), 128; S. E. Smart, "The Take-up and Renewal of Rent Rebates by GLC Tenants," *Housing Monthly* (July 1975), 26.

7. Cited by Marion Steele in her unpublished study of housing allowances, Chap. 5, 9.

8. Freda Cocks, "Housing Allowances for Private Tenants: Birmingham's Experiences," *Housing Review* (January-February 1972), 24.

9. Ira S. Lowry, *Experimenting With Housing Allowances* (Santa Monica: Rand Corporation, 1982), Executive Summary, v.

10. Stephen D. Kennedy and Jean MacMillian, *Participation Under Alternative Housing Allowance Programs: Evidence From the Housing Allowance Demand Experiment* (Cambridge, MA: Abt Associates, 1980), S-2

11. Robert L. Walker, *Canvassing Rent Allowances in Bristol and Westminster* (London: Housing Development Directorate, Department of Environment, ca. 1978).

12. William L. Holshouser, Jr., "The Role of Supportive Services" in *The Great Housing Experiment*, eds., Joseph Friedman and Daniel H. Weinberg (Beverly Hills, CA: Sage Publications, 1983), 116-21.

13. Belgium, Housing and Family Welfare Administration, *Social Housing Policy in Belgium* (Germantown, MD: HUD USER, 1969), 63-64.

14. Sweden, Housing Subsidy Committee, *Housing Subsidies* (Germantown, MD: HUD USER, 1982), 29-30.

15. France, Jacques Badet (Chairman), *Report of the Working Group on the Reform of Personal Housing Assistance* (Germantown, MD: HUD USER, 1982), 14.

16. *Ibid.*, 121.

17. Finland, Ministry of Environment, *A Report of a Comparative Analysis of Three Finnish Housing Allowance Systems* (Helsinki: Ministry of Environment, 1985), 11, published only in Finnish; information provided by Keijo Tanner, National Housing Board, January 12, 1985.

18. Stephen K. Mayo and Jorn Barnbrock, *Rental Housing Subsidy Programs in Germany and the U.S.: A Comparative Program Evaluation* (Bonn: Bundesministerium fur Bauwesen, Raumordnung und Stadtebau, 1980), 36.

19. Freda Cocks, "Housing Allowances for Private Tenants—Birmingham's Experiences," *Housing Review* (January-February 1972), 25.

6

Formulas for Calculating Housing Allowances

The preceding chapters analyzed the major factors governments have considered in setting up their housing allowance systems. This chapter examines two broad formulas from which housing allowance systems may choose, and then summarizes the formulas that governments have adopted for calculating their housing allowances. The notation systems used in the national formulas have been simplified and converted to a uniform notation system to facilitate the reader in comparing the basic principles applied in the various formulas.

Bridging the Gap—Some Theoretical Models

The central issue in housing subsidy policy today is the gap between what workers can afford to pay for shelter and what they must pay for decent accommodations in the housing market, that is, the affordability problem. How can the gap most effectively be bridged?

Assuming that the gap is bridged by some form of housing allowance, there are two broad alternatives.[1] The first method is to determine the actual rent which is the monthly cost of decent housing and subtract from that what the family can afford to pay expressed as a percentage of income. Quantitative values can be assigned to these two variables without difficulty. The lower the income, the less the family can afford to pay. As family income rises, the gap decreases, and the amount of supplementary income needed declines correspondingly until zero is reached. The larger the family, the higher the cost of decent housing, and so also the greater the gap for families within a given income range. The larger the gap, the higher the allowance must be to serve its purpose. The allowance may cover the total difference between the actual rent and what the family can afford to pay, or it may cover only a fraction of that difference. The system is independent of rent levels, and has the strong ethical value of promoting horizontal equity among households, that is, households at the same income level bear relatively the same burden of rent.

The housing gap formula is expressed graphically in Figure 1 and algebraically in the following equation:

Housing allowance $= R - aY$

where:

R   is the actual rent or cost of decent housing normally subject to a ceiling;

Y   is household income normally adjusted in some way or another and subject to a ceiling; and

a   is the reasonable shelter-to-income ratio (SIR), that is, the percentage of income that the family can afford to pay, as determined legislatively or administratively.

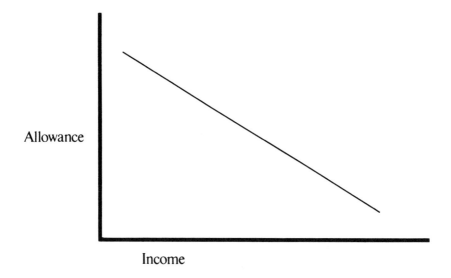

Figure 1.   Graphic Representation of the Housing Gap Formula

A second general method of designing a housing allowance is to calculate it as a percent of rent. The rationale is that the higher the rent, the greater the financial burden on the household budget, and the greater the need for housing subsidy. The payment formula is independent of income and family size and is geared directly to the size of the rent. This formula has the disadvantage of encouraging overconsumption of housing by paying the highest allowance to families which have the highest rents.

This method, called the percent-of-rent formula, is expressed graphically in Figure 2 and algebraically in the following equation:

Housing allowance = bR

where:

    b   is the percent of rent payable in the form of a housing allowance as determined legislatively or administratively; and

    R   is actual monthly rent normally subject to a ceiling.

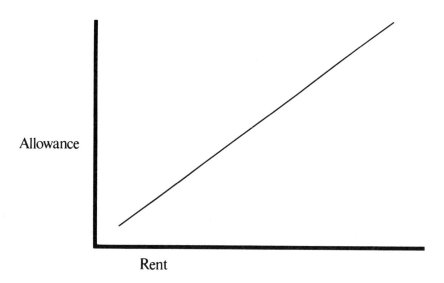

Figure 2. Graphic Representation of the Percent-of-Rent Formula

A third interesting concept has been put forward by Janet McClain, Housing Program Director of the Canadian Council on Social Development; in this concept, the housing allowance should be introduced as a shelter tax credit, or alternatively as an occupancy cost rebate.[2] The idea is to develop a global, prorated income tax system that provides a monthly tax rebate tied to rent collection. Since many, if not most, low-income families have zero income for tax purposes, and hence often do not bother to file income tax forms, such a program would have to be extensively publicized to ensure that needy households obtain their tax credits.

Australia

Australia adopted a rent rebate plan for public housing tenants in 1945 and broadened the system in 1969. After wide discussion in the 1970s, the government published in 1978 a detailed proposal for a three-year housing allowance experiment that would have involved 3,750 families. Although this plan was never implemented, the proposed formula for calculating the housing allowance is of interest.

The formula chosen for the demonstration project was as follows:[3]

Housing allowance $= bR - aY$

where:

R is the rent paid subject to a ceiling;
Y is household income;
a is the rate at which payment is reduced as income increases; and
b is the proportion of rent paid as a subsidy.

The experiment was designed to test three different levels of subsidizing housing consumption for two different factors in order to measure consumer response. The two factors were: (1) various percentages of income that were believed to be reasonable shelter-to-income ratios; and (2) various percentages of the rents actually paid.

The maximum fair SIR for one group was set at 16 percent, for a second group at 20 percent, and for a third group at 25 percent. This was factor "a" in the formula. Similarly the amount of the rent actually paid that was to be subsidized was to be tested in each of the three groups at 100 percent for the first category, 80 percent for the second category, and 64 percent for the third category. This was factor "b" in the formula.

Maximum rent levels determined the point at which participating households would be financially supported. This level was defined as the "rent level for adequate accommodation in an average suburb, depending on the size and basic needs of the different families involved."[4] The key factor in determining the maximum rent was the number of bedrooms required according to the following rules:

1. One bedroom for each married or *de facto* couple;
2. one bedroom for each other person aged 18 or over;
3. one bedroom for each two persons aged 10 to 17 years and of the same sex;
4. any person aged 10 to 17 years left over after this pairing was paired with a child under 10 of the same sex, or if this kind of pairing was not possible, such person was given a separate bedroom; and
5. any remaining children under 10 years were paired, and a bedroom was given to each pair and to any remaining child.

The dollar amounts of the various rent ceilings were then determined by rent surveys.

For the purpose of this experiment, it was decided that income would be:

1. Gross income from employment, property, and business;
2. less expenses incurred in earning that income, as would be normally admitted by the Commissioner of Taxation;
3. plus all government benefits except maternity and handicapped child allowances;
4. plus gifts or *ex gratia* payments from other persons.

Finally, only households with a total income below \$286 (A\$250; 1978) a week were eligible to apply.

Austria

In the early 1960s several provinces adopted housing allowance systems, but it was not until 1968 that federal action was taken. Under the decentralized government structure, there are considerable provincial differences in the administration of the national system.

The general formula for calculating the allowance is:[5]

Housing allowance $= R - R_r$

where:

R   is the actual rent; and

R_r is the reasonable rent which the household should pay.

The reasonable rent is in turn a function of two variables—the level of family income and the number of members in the household—the formula for which is as follows:

$$R_r = f(Y, M)$$

where:

Y   is net family income, including transfer payments such as family allowances; and

M   is number of members of the household.

The national system requires that provinces determine the percentage of income which each household must pay for shelter at different income levels and for different size families within income ceilings. These SIRs are then issued in tables prepared by the provinces. The percentages range from 0 percent in Vienna for households with four or more occupants in the lowest income groups (that is, households with monthly incomes of less than $80 [AS2,000] in 1971) to 25 percent for single member households in the highest income groups within the income ceilings in the provinces of Carinthia and Lower Austria (that is, households with monthly incomes of over $240 [AS6,000] in 1971). The housing allowance is then the difference between the actual rent and the reasonable rent that a household should pay.

The following example is given of the calculation of the allowance in 1971:[6]

1. Gross income:

a.	wages	AS107,085.00
b.	housing allowance	360.00
c.	family allowance	6,440.00
	Total	113,885.00

2. Deductions:

a.	nontaxable portion of gross income (exceptional payments, additional payments, bonuses)	4,056.90

b.	income tax, including contributions	5,496.00
c.	other deductions—social security, contributions to workmen's associations, contributions for the promotion of building	9,625.15
d.	other nontaxable sums	14,532.00
e.	contractual expenses for publicity	3,276.00
f.	contractual expenses of an exceptional nature	3,276.00
	Total	AS40,262.14

3. Net income on which the housing allowance is based: AS73,623.00

The published tables then indicate the amount of rent paid and the allowance received for a household with an income of $2,950 (AS73,623.46).

Canada

For more than a decade the housing allowance issue has been much debated in Canada. Although the national government has not yet adopted a freestanding housing allowance system, a rent supplement has been incorporated in the National Housing Act program. Without waiting for national action, five provinces—British Columbia, Manitoba, New Brunswick, Nova Scotia, and Quebec—adopted their own plans in the 1970s/1980s, mainly for the elderly. The British Columbia Shelter Aid for Elderly Renters Program (SAFER) may be regarded as typical.

The SAFER formula is as follows:[7]

Housing allowance $= 0.75 (R - 0.30Y)$

where:

R is actual rent subject to a ceiling; and
Y is family income within a ceiling.

The reason for paying 75 percent rather than 100 percent of the gap is to provide an incentive for economy in the amount of housing services purchased.

The formula operates within rent ceilings, which in 1978 were $180 (C$205) for single persons, and $197 (C$225) for couples. However, elderly persons who pay over 30 percent of income on rent are not automatically disqualified if rent payments exceed rent ceilings. But in the calculation of the housing allowance, no account is taken of the amount of rent above the ceiling. Tables have been prepared to show participants what their allowances will be, taking into account their incomes and their rents.

The federal rent supplement provision under the National Housing Act program is based on the following formula:[8]

Rent supplement $= R - aY$

where:

R is actual costs, including all capital and operating costs;
Y is adjusted household income; and
a is the reasonable shelter-to-income ratio ranging from 16.7 to 25 percent.

In the administration of the rent supplement, provinces have introduced their own variations.

Denmark

In Denmark there are two housing allowance systems, one for families and one for pensioners. For the most part, both systems follow the same method of calculation.

The basic formula for the pensioner system is as follows:[9]

Housing allowance $= R - aY - D$

where:

R is actual rent;
Y is household income with an annual ceiling in 1981 of $10,458 (DK74,500);
D is a "deduction factor" which reduces the amount of the allowance if the actual rent is above a prescribed rent per square meter; and
a is the reasonable shelter-to-income ratio on a progressive scale, taking into account the level of income, the number of children, and the size of the dwelling.

The sum "aY" is called the "residual rent" (in our terminology the "reasonable rent") which every household must pay. Under the law, the Ministry of Housing publishes tables showing "residual rents" for all categories of households.

The maximum rent paid on ceiling income is 15 percent. As the annual income declines, and as the size of the family increases, the required SIR declines. For example, for a couple with four children and an income of $3,597 (DK25,000) in 1972, the ratio was one-half the ratio of a couple in the same income bracket with no children.

The major difference between the two Danish systems is in the treatment of the gap between the actual rent and the residual rent. In the case of pensioners the housing allowance covers the total gap; for non-pensioner households, the government pays only 75 percent of the gap.

Federal Republic of Germany

The German housing allowance plan was launched in 1955. It received a major overhaul in 1965 and again in 1977 when 300,000 additional households came under the plan. In its initial proposal, the government embraced the principle of covering 100 percent of the gap between the actual rent and "bearable" housing expenditures. But as noted in Chapter 3 (Unaffordable Gap to Be Covered by Subsidy), this concept was abandoned.

The general formula for calculating the allowance is as follows: [10]

Housing allowance $= G (R - R_r)$

where:

G is the percent of the gap between actual rent and reasonable rent which the allowance is designed to cover, statutorily determined, decreasing with income and increasing with family size within the limits of 0.05 and 0.22;

R is the actual household rent; and

R_r is the reasonable rent which the participant is expected to pay.

The reasonable rent is in turn a function of four variables—the level of family income; the number of members of the household; the size of the urban community; and the date of construction—the formula for which is:

$R_r = f (Y, M, U, Z)$

where:

Y   is family income;
M   is the number of members of the household;
U   is the size of the urban area in which the dwelling is located, of which there are three categories:

Those less than 100,000 population;
those from 100,000 to 500,000 population; and
those over 500,000 population; and

Z   is date of construction, of which there are three periods:

Dwelling units constructed before December 31, 1965;
dwelling units constructed between December 31, 1965, and December 31, 1971; and
dwelling units constructed after December 31, 1971.

The Ministry for Land Development, Construction, and Urbanization has prepared a book of tables showing housing allowances payable, taking into account all the above variables.

Rent, for the purposes of the act, includes charges for a number of related housing services, including water, sewage, garbage disposal, and electricity for staircase lights. In the case of homeowners, certain maintenance and operating costs are included in addition to payments on mortgage principal and interest. If rents and related charges are within the rent ceilings that are administratively determined, then the family is entitled to a rent allowance.

The system has a special concept of "family income" derived in the following manner. All income received by members of the family, including unemployment and sickness benefits, and social security payments, is totaled. Certain deductions, such as child support payments, normal tax deductible items, and exemptions for certain groups of persons, are then made from gross family income. This amount is then reduced automatically by a certain percentage—15, 22.5, or 30 percent—depending on whether members of the family are working and paying taxes and/or social security contributions. This is to maintain equity between working participants who pay certain taxes and nonworking participants who do not pay such taxes. This adjusted amount represents "family income" as defined in the act. If the family income is below the income ceiling as defined administratively, then the family qualifies for a housing allowance. For example, for a four-person family the monthly income ceiling in 1978 was $926 (DM1,860).

The following example is given of a typical housing allowance for a couple with two children in 1978:[11]

> Income: both spouses have income, both pay social security contributions and taxes on their income;
>
> Housing: they live in a rented apartment, completed in 1966, equipped with district heating and bath;
>
> Location: city with 300,000 inhabitants.

Monthly income (including child support payment):

	Husband	Wife
Gross income	DM1,748.43	DM475.57
Less normal deductible sum	47.00	47.00
Less exemption for children	130.00	–
	1,571.43	428.57
Less lump sum deduction (30 percent)	471.43	128.57
	DM1,100.00	DM300.00
Total family income	DM1,400 or $697	
Monthly rent to be paid		DM420
Monthly rent to which housing allowance is applicable (maximum DM480)		DM420
Monthly housing allowance		DM80

The housing allowance of $40 (DM80) is derived from the housing allowance table for a four-person family with a monthly income between DM1,380 and DM1,400 and a monthly rent between DM400 and DM420.

Finland

Finland adopted its first housing allowance plan in 1941. Today there are three different systems for renters and owners: one for families and single persons; a supplementary housing allowance for pensioners; and supplementary housing support to university students.

The basic formula for the general system is as follows:[12]

$$\text{Housing allowance} = \frac{80}{100} \times (R_s - B)$$

where:

R_s is the approved housing expenditure according to the size of the household and as determined by the State Council; and

B   is the basic part of the rent which the household must pay as specified by the State Council, the formula for which is as follows:

$$\frac{aY + R_s \times (80 - 100)}{80}$$

where:

Y is monthly household income within an income ceiling, ranging from $803 (FM4,470) for a single-person household to $1,619 (FM9,020) for a family of four to $2,623 (FM14,610; 1983) for a family of eight; and

a is the reasonable shelter-to-income ratio which the family is expected to pay, ranging from 10.8 percent for an eight-person family with a monthly income of $359 (FM2,000) to 22 percent for a four-person household with a monthly income of $2,460 (FM13,750; 1983).

"R_s", the approved housing expenditure, is in effect a rent ceiling and therefore different from the actual market rent. It establishes an upper rent limit per square meter (m^2) for floor space, taking into consideration (1) the amount of floor space deemed reasonable for the household to have in light of the number of persons, and (2) the characteristics of the dwelling, such as age, location, equipment, and heating system. For example, the reasonable useful floor space of a dwelling varies from 35 m² (377 square feet) for a single-person household to 90 m² (969 square feet) for a four-person household to 135 m² (1,453 square feet) for an eight-person household.

There are three ways to express the amount of the housing allowance which the government pays. The first way is that the subsidy is equal to 80 percent of the difference between the approved housing expenditure and the basic part of the rent as defined. The second way is that the subsidy is equal to the difference between the approved housing expenditure and the sum of the basic part of the rent and another part of the rent which is termed "additional part," the formula for which is as follows:

$$\frac{80}{100} \times (R_s - B)$$

The third way is that the subsidy is equal to the difference between the approved housing expenditure and the reasonable shelter-to-income ratio times monthly gross household income (that is, "aY").

The system also has a wealth ceiling. The limit ranges between $21,544 and $28,725 (FM120,000 to FM160,000; 1983), depending on the number of household members.[13]

France

The first French housing allowance was adopted in 1948 as supplementary support to the family allowance system for both renters and owners. A second system was instituted in 1971 for the elderly, the physically handicapped, and young workers. Following the 1975 recommendations of the National Commission to Study a Reform of the Financing of Housing (headed by Raymond Barre, later Prime Minister), the government adopted a third comprehensive housing allowance system in 1977 called "L'Aide Personnalisee au Logement," marking a major change of direction in national housing policy. In contrast to the earlier housing allowance systems which were adopted as a social housing policy, the so-called individualized housing subsidy was conceived as an economic assistance policy.

The formula governing the calculation of the new housing allowance system is as follows:[14]

Housing allowance = K (R + C − R$_r$)

where:

R   is the actual rent subject to a ceiling;
C   represents certain amenities in high-rise
     buildings;
R_r is the reasonable or minimum rent; and
K   is a weighting factor.

"R," the rent, is determined by geographical location and size of family. There are three geographical zones: (1) Zone I, consisting of Greater Paris; (2) Zone II, composed of all cities over 100,000 population; and (3) Zone III, covering all other areas. For renters, the rent level in 1977 was fixed at $162 (FF800) per month; for homeowners living in housing built by the social housing, nonprofit organization called HLM, the rent was also FF800 a month; but for owners living in unsubsidized housing financed by conventional private market mortgages, the rent ceiling was increased to $224 (FF1,100).

The symbol "C" refers to the cost of certain quality features of modern urban housing construction such as elevators. The formula permits the addition of up to $20 (FF100) a month to the allowable rent to cover the additional expenses involved in modern conveniences ("certains elements du confort moderne"), which French housing policy seeks to encourage.

"R_r" represents the reasonable or minimum rent which the household should be expected to pay, taking into account its taxable income and the number of children. Taxable income has been arbitrarily set at 72 percent of gross income, the difference of 28 percent being assumed to cover such items as income and social security taxes. Transfer payments, such as family allowances, are considered as taxable income. Reasonable rent is therefore a function of the level of family income and the number of members of the family, the formula for which is as follows:

$$R_r = f\,(Y, M)$$

where:

Y   is family income; and
M   is the number of members of the family.

Due account of taxable income is taken by calculating the following sum: zero percent of all the income in the first layer of taxable income; 15 percent of the second layer of taxable income; 28 percent of the third layer of taxable income; and 40 percent of the fourth layer of taxable income. The magnitude of the four layers is determined by the number of persons in the household: the larger the number of persons, the larger the size of each layer of income, as indicated in the following examples:

Layers of Taxable Income in French Francs (1977)

	1st layer	2nd layer	3rd layer	4th layer
Family with no children	0-3,000	3,000- 6,000	6,000-12,000	above 12,000
Family with two children	0-5,000	5,100-10,200	10,200-20,400	above 20,400

As an illustration, a family with two children having a 1977 annual taxable income of $4,477 (FF22,000) would have had the following annual rent to pay: (FF5,100 × 0) + (FF5,100 × 15 percent) + (FF10,200 × 28 percent) + (FF1,600 × 40 percent) = FF4,261 or $867.

The final symbol in the formula, "K," introduces a weighting factor, the purpose of which is to reduce the gap between actual rent and reasonable rent that is covered by the housing allowance. The weighting factor is fixed by administrative regulation, with the coefficient varying between 0.65 and 0.95. This value is derived from the following formula:

$$K = 0.95 - \frac{Y}{80,000 \times N}$$

where:

Y   is total taxable income; and

N   is an assigned value based on the number of persons in the household according to the following scale:

Single person	— 0.8
Couple without child	— 1.0
Couple with child	— 1.35
Household with 2 children	— 1.7
Household with 3 children	— 2.2
Household with 4 children	— 2.65
Each child above 4	— an additional 0.35

Netherlands

The Dutch housing allowance was introduced in 1970. It was viewed as a central pillar in national housing policy in achieving the larger objectives of increasing and harmonizing rents in the national housing market and in reducing producer housing subsidies. The system was greatly expanded in scope in 1975—doubling the number of participants—when an expanded, mixed consumer and producer housing subsidy program was launched.

The basic housing gap formula is:[15]

Housing allowance $= R - aY - D$

where:

R   is the actual market rent within a ceiling;

Y   is taxable household income;

D   is a "deduction factor" which reduces the amount of the allowance if the actual rent is above the rent ceiling; and

a   is the reasonable shelter-to-income ratio as determined administratively by the Ministry of Housing and Physical Planning on a progressive scale, ranging from 11.63 percent for workers at the minimum annual wage level (i.e., $7,500, FL22,500) to 21.57 percent for workers at the wage ceiling (i.e., $13,000, FL39,000; 1983).

Multiplying taxable household income by the reasonable SIR yields, in Dutch terminology, the "standard rent," or in the terminology and notation followed in this study (in order to facilitate international comparability), "reasonable rent" (R_r). Accordingly, the Ministry has prepared a table showing reasonable rents at all pay levels covered by the housing allowance system.

This formula, which covers 100 percent of the gap between the actual rent (R) and reasonable rent (R_r), is, however, applicable only for tenants living in very low-rent accommodation—defined in 1983-84 as dwellings in which both "R" and "R_r" were below $1,320 (FL3,960). If "R" exceeds the minimum rent of FL3,960, then the housing allowance ceases to cover 100 percent of the gap, and a series of more complicated formulas are then applicable, depending on the participant's level of income and of rent.

The simplest expression of the formula, which covers less than 100 percent of the gap, is:

Housing allowance $= R - aY - (R-3960) \times K$

where:

R   is the actual rent;
Y   is taxable income;
a   is the reasonable shelter-to-income ratio; and
K   is an administratively determined coefficient, ranging from zero for tenants in the minimum wage bracket to 0.35 percent for persons in the highest wage bracket covered by the housing allowance system.

The Dutch formula thus incorporates the principle of progressivity (that is, the principle of ability to pay) into the housing allowance formula in two ways. First, it adopts a progressive scale in establishing reasonable shelter-to-income ratios. Second, the reimbursable percentage of the gap between actual rents and reasonable rents is lowered as the tenant's income increases up to the income ceiling.

The government has imposed these limitations on the percent of gap coverage in its housing allowance system in order to keep its program financial commitments from expanding unduly.

Norway

Starting with a limited rent subsidy plan in the early 1960s, the government extended the system substantially in 1972 with two main objectives: to assist families with well-below-average incomes; and to mitigate hardship for families which had to accept much more expensive, recently built housing. The expanded program made a more specific link between income and housing expenses for both owners and renters.

The formula for calculating the housing allowance is:[16]

Housing allowance $= 0.70 \, (R - R_r)$

where:

R   is actual rent as calculated partly accordingly to fixed rules promulgated by the Ministry and partly according to rates established in the housing market; and

R_r is "reasonable rent," which is a function of the level of family income and the number of members of the household, the formula for which is:

$$R_r = f(Y, M)$$

where:

Y   is family income; and
M   is the number of family members.

A table has been developed showing income ceilings for households varying from one member to six persons or more. Another table establishes housing expenditure ceilings, ranging from one member per family to five persons or more. For low-income households, 15 percent is considered a reasonable shelter-to-income ratio. This percentage rises to a ceiling of 20 percent.

The Norwegian system has an interesting incentive for households to occupy larger space. The minimum rent that a housing allowance recipient must pay may be reduced by 10 percent for each room in excess of the following standards:

1 person	—	3 rooms and kitchen;
2 and 3 persons	—	4 rooms and kitchen;
4 and 5 persons	—	5 rooms and kitchen.

The following example is given showing the calculation of the housing allowance for the first six months of 1976:[17]

Dwelling:	single-family house constructed in 1973 consisting of four rooms and kitchen;
Family:	four persons, including two children;
Income:	total household income—$7,515 (NK41,008);
Location:	municipality of Ringsaker.

Housing expenses:

Interest, National Housing Board first mortgage	NK2,007
Installment on National Housing Board mortgage	430
Interest, down payment	529
Installment down payment	1,080
Municipality tax	225
Operating cost	350
Real estate tax	0
Leasehold tax (land rent)	0
	4,621

Reasonable rent:

$$\frac{43,008 \times 17}{2 \times 100}$$

	3,656
Difference	NK965

Rent allowance:

$$\frac{965 \times 70}{100}$$

NK676 or $123

Sweden

Swedish housing allowances have been available to families with children since the 1930s. In the post-World War II period up to 1969, the computation of the allowance was dependent on four factors: the number of children; housing standards; family income; and rent levels. In 1969 a new law was adopted to strengthen the economic support of all needy families with children.

In the 1970s all requirements relating to the size and equipment of the dwelling were abolished. In 1974 the system was extended to include low-income families without children. Sweden now has three types of housing allowances: a national plan; a combined national and municipal system based on income and housing costs; and a municipal housing allowance system supplementing the national pension system.

The national-municipal system is governed by the following formula:[18]

Housing allowance $= G (R - R_r)$

where:

R   is actual rent within a rent ceiling;

R_r is the reasonable rent, which in Swedish terminology is "the lower cost threshold" that is established administratively by the Ministry of Housing and Physical Planning within appropriate income ceilings; and

G   is the percentage of gap coverage, ranging up to 80 percent.

Reasonable rent, R_r, is in turn dependent on two variables: income, and the number of members of the household. That is,

$$R_r = f(Y, M)$$

where:

M   is the number of members of household; and
Y   is annual 1984 family income within the fol-
      lowing limits:

Single person without children	$3,093 (SK26,000)
Married/unmarried couples without children	$3,330 (SK28,000)
Single person with children	$4,163 (SK35,000)
Couples with children	$5,114 (SK43,000)

As regards income, the applicant must pass a means test based on taxable income set by the national government but administered by the municipality. If the participant holds assets these are taken into consideration.

The full housing allowance, that is, 80 percent of the gap between actual rent and reasonable rent, is payable when the participant's income does not exceed the above limits. For that part of the qualifying income which exceeds the above limits, the allowance is reduced by 15 percent up to an upper income limit of $7,731 (SK65,000), beyond which the reduction is at the rate of 22 percent, tapering off to 100 percent at the overall ceiling limits (which in April 1984 for a family with two children, for example, was $13,321 [SK112,000]).

On April 1, 1984, the maximum unreduced annual housing allowances were as follows:

Single person without children	$171 (SK 1,440)
Married/unmarried couples without children	$343 (SK 2,880)
Family with one child	$1,493 (SK12,540)
Family with two children	$1,871 (SK15,720)
Family with three children	$2,666 (SK23,460)
Family with four children	$3,171 (SK26,640)
Family with five children	$4,035 (SK33,900)
For each additional child	$379 (SK 3,180)

Switzerland (Basle Canton)

Although the federal government has not yet adopted a national plan, Basle Canton and Zurich city have had housing allowance systems for large families and the elderly since the late 1950s and early 1960s. The Basle large family plan for three or more children will be taken as representative of the Swiss point of view.

The Basle formula is constructed as follows: [19]

Housing allowance $= G(R - aY) + X$

where:

R   is the household shelter cost including for renters the actual rent plus costs of repairs up to a specified amount and for homeowners the actual expense allowed for rental property or the taxable rental value of the dwelling;

Y   is the gross income of all members residing in the household plus one-tenth of the total wealth of the household in excess of the wealth ceiling (as indicated by the most recent assessment for the cantonal tax), with deductions allowed for each underage child, contributions to the Old Age and Surviving Dependents Insurance Fund, and certain portions of the income received by the wife and children;

a   is the reasonable percent of household income that the participant should pay, beginning with a maximum of 15 percent for families with three children and declining with each additional child;

G   is the percent of the gap between actual rent and the reasonable rent which the allowance is designed to cover, that is, between 10 and 40 percent; and

X   is an extra allowance, ranging from 25 to 50 percent of that portion of shelter costs which exceeds one-fifth of family income.

United Kingdom

From the beginning of Council housing (that is, public housing), local authorities have had power to give rent rebates on such terms "as they may think fit." In the early 1970s, about two-thirds of the local authorities operated rent rebate systems. In 1972 the government adopted a systematic national policy requiring local authorities to provide rent rebates to all qualified Council housing tenants and rent allowances to all qualified private tenants.

The British housing allowance system is built around the concept of the household's basic living expenses, including the income tax and national insurance payments of an employed person. These expenses are calculated by the administrative agency and are termed the "needs allowance." In 1980 the weekly needs allowance for a single person was $80 (£34.90), for a married couple $120 (£51.70), for a couple or single person and a child $142 (£61.30), plus $22 (£9.60) for each additional child.

If household income equals the needs allowance, the tenant pays a minimum rent equal to 40 percent of the actual rent. If household income exceeds the needs allowance, the tenant pays a minimum rent equal to 40 percent of the actual rent plus 17 percent of the excess.[20] If household income falls below the needs allowance, then the tenant pays a minimum rent equal to 40 percent of the actual rent minus 25 percent of the shortfall. If necessary the minimum rent may fall to zero.

The general formula can therefore be written as follows:[21]

Housing allowance $= R - R_r$

where:

R is actual rent; and
R_r is the reasonable or minimum rent which the household is expected to pay.

The formulas for the three categories of minimum weekly rent (i.e., R_r) are then:

(1) When $Y = N$
     minimum rent $= 0.40\ R$;
(2) When $Y > N$
     minimum rent $= 0.40\ R + 0.17\ (Y - N)$; and R
(3) When $Y < N$
     minimum rent $= 0.40\ R - 0.25\ (N - Y)$

where:

Y is household income; and
N is the needs allowance.

The amount of the rent allowance is then equal to the difference between the actual rent and the minimum rent calculated according to the above formula. In 1980 the maximum rent allowance in London was $58 (£25) and elsewhere $53 (£23).

United States

The United States spent $150 million on its Experimental Housing Allowance Program (EHAP) over the ten years 1973–1982. The program was divided into three major tracks: two demonstration sites to test the household demand response to housing allowances over a three-year period; two sites to measure the market supply response to housing allowances over a ten-year period; and eight sites to examine the administration of a housing allowance program and the costs associated with its delivery over a two-year to three-year period.

Building on EHAP experience, in 1974 the so-called Section 8 Program adopted a modified form of the housing allowance.[22] It pays a monthly stipend to landlords of privately owned, existing housing on behalf of the tenant that covers the difference between the actual market rent and 25 percent of the household's adjusted income. The tenant chooses the location; the dwelling unit must meet HUD's housing quality standards; and rent must not exceed fair market rent, that is, the typical price for a modest rental unit for families of various sizes as set by the Department of Housing and Urban Development. In 1981 the shelter-to-income ratio was raised from 25 to 30 percent. When other forms of Section 8 assistance are added, an estimated total of around 2,139,000 lower income households will receive payments in 1985.

In 1984 Congress adopted a new Housing Voucher Program that differs from the Section 8 Existing Program in three important ways. First, the voucher is the difference between the fair market rent (not the actual rent) and 30 percent of adjusted household income. This provides an incentive for the tenant to shop around and find the lowest rent on minimum-standard housing. Second, a tenant is able to select housing at higher than a fair market rent, and then pay the difference out of his own pocket. Third, payment standards have been liberalized for large families. One part of the Housing Voucher Program operates as a supplement to the Rental Rehabilitation Grant Program, and the other "freestanding" part is to be paid out to 4,543 households in 20 cities under a new demonstration program administered by local public housing authorities. Eligibility is limited to very-low-income families, i.e., those below 50 percent of the median income of the area where they live.[23]

The EHAP formula governing the housing allowances paid to around 20,000 households in the housing supply experiment was:[24]

Housing allowance $= R_s - .25Y$

where:

    R_s was the estimated "standard cost of adequate housing" determined by market surveys for each size household; and

    Y   was the adjusted household income.

The EHAP demand experiment tested essentially two different payment formulas: the housing gap formula; and the percent-of-rent formula.[25] The formula applying the housing gap method to around 3,000 households was:

Housing allowance $= R_s - bY$

where:

    R_s was the estimated cost of modest existing standard housing at each site according to household size as set by HUD mainly on the basis of market surveys; and

    b   was the rate at which the allowance was reduced as income increased.

Households participating in the EHAP Housing Gap Plan could only receive payments if they rented units that met certain housing requirements. Three different sets of requirements were tested—one minimum standards requirement and two minimum rent requirements. Under the minimum standard requirement, households qualified for payments if their dwelling unit met certain physical requirements and occupancy standards.

Under the minimum rent requirements, households qualified for payments if they spent at least a certain minimum amount for rent. The two minimum rent requirements tested were minimum rent low, under which households had to spend at least 70 percent of the estimated cost of standard housing on rent, and minimum rent high, under which households had to spend at least 90 percent of the estimated cost of standard housing on rent. The intent of the minimum rent requirements was to ensure that households spent enough for rent to obtain decent housing, while allowing them flexibility with respect to specific unit features and location. If rent proved to be highly correlated with housing quality, then a minimum rent level would provide a simple method of assuring minimum standard housing without the administrative problems and costs of actually verifying this fact by inspections. As indicated in Chapter 4 (Physical Structure), neither of the minimum rent concepts proved to be a good proxy for minimum physical standards.

The EHAP formula applying the percent-of-rent formula to around 1,600 households was:

Housing allowance $=$ aR

where:

R   was household rent; and
a   was the fraction of the rent paid by the housing allowance system.

Five rebate levels were tested for "a": 0.2, 0.3, 0.4, 0.5, and 0.6. Thus, a household in the 0.5 rebate group could rent any dwelling unit in the program at one-half its market cost. The formula was tested as a means of measuring demand elasticities. It was not intended that it would ever be applied in a real program without some provision for a declining fraction of the rent gap to be covered as the income of the participant rose.

Summary

The formulas of the various housing allowance systems are summarized in Table 8. No attempt is made to present the systems in all their complexities; only the basic formula is reproduced.

To facilitate comparisons among the many systems, the national formulas have been converted to the following uniform system of notation:

where:

R   is the actual market rent;
R_s is the rent of a modest standard dwelling unit, that is, an approved rent or a fair market rent as determined by the appropriate housing body;
R_r is the reasonable rent that the household may be expected to pay taking all factors into consideration;
Y   is family income (e.g., taxable or adjusted income);
M   is the number of members in the family;
D   is a "deduction factor" which reduces the amount of the allowance if the actual rent is above the rent ceiling;
U   is the size of the urban area in which the dwelling is located;
Z   is the date of construction of the dwelling unit;

G   is the percentage of the gap between actual rent and reasonable rent that is covered by the allowance;

X   is an extra allowance that covers a portion of shelter costs exceeding one-fifth of family income;

B   is the basic part of rent which the household must pay;

C   is certain amenities in high-rise apartment buildings;

K   is a coefficient legislatively or administratively determined;

a   is the reasonable shelter-to-income ratio (SIR); and

b   is the percent of rent.

TABLE 8
Summary of Housing Allowance Formulas of Highly Industrialized Countries

Country	Formula
1. Australia (Proposed demonstration project)	$bR - aY$
2. Austria	$R - R_r$ where $R_r = f(Y, M)$
3. Canada (British Columbia)	$0.75 (R - 0.30Y)$
4. Denmark	$R - aY - D$
5. Finland	$0.80 (R_s - B)$
6. France	$K (R + C - R_r)$ where $R_r = f(Y, M)$
7. Federal Republic of Germany, the	$G (R - R_r)$ where $R_r = f(Y, M, U, Z)$
8. Netherlands, the	$R - aY - D$
9. Norway	$0.70 (R - R_r)$ where $R_r = f(Y, M)$
10. Sweden	$G (R - R_r)$ where $R_r = f(Y, M)$
11. Switzerland (Basle Canton)	$G (R - aY) + X$
12. United Kingdom	$R - R_r$ where $R_r = 0.40R$
13. United States EHAP Supply Experiment (1)	$R_s - 0.25Y$
EHAP Demand Experiment (2)	$R_s - bY$
(2b)	aR

It is clear that the great majority of housing allowance systems have adopted the housing gap formula approach. The systems vary considerably, however, as regards the definition of actual rent, the concept of approved rent, the definition of reasonable shelter-to-income ratios, and the percentage of coverage between reasonable rents and actual rents.

NOTES

1. Carlton and Ferreira distinguish three additional hybrid subtypes of formulas combining characteristics of these basic methods, and they have tested the behavior of all five models in a 10-year simulation using the Pittsburgh, Pennsylvania, metropolitan housing market 1960-70 data base. Dennis W. Carlton and Joseph Ferreira, Jr., "Selecting Subsidy Strategies for Housing Allowance Programs," *Journal of Urban Economics*, Vol. 4 (1977), 221-47. *See also* K. F. Watson, F. Ermuth, and W. Hamilton, *A Comparative Analysis of Housing Allowance Programs* (Ottawa: Canada Mortgage and Housing Corporation, 1978), 8-17. Denton, Robb, and Spencer distinguish three main types of formulas: gap formula; rent proportion formula; and cash transfer formula. They then run computer simulations testing consumer behavior under many different assumptions. Frank T. Denton, A. Leslie Robb, and Byron G. Spencer, *The Economics of Shelter Allowances* (Ottawa: Canada Mortgage and Housing Corporation, 1982), 5.

2. Janet McClain, ed., *Are Housing Allowances the Answer?* (Ottawa: Canadian Council on Social Development, 1979), 12-14.

3. Australia, Department of Environment, Housing and Community Development, *Housing Allowance Experiment: Final Design* (Canberra: Department of Environment, Housing and Community Development, 1978), Vol. 1, 11-13.

4. *Ibid.*, 5.

5. N. Zeyl, "Systems of Individual Subsidies" in United Nations Economic Commission for Europe, Committee on Housing, Building and Planning, *Financing of Housing* (Geneva: United Nations Economic Commission for Europe, 1973), 168.

6. *Ibid.*, 172.

7. British Columbia, Ministry of Municipal Affairs and Housing, *Profile of the SAFER Beneficiaries* (Vancouver: Ministry of Municipal Affairs and Housing, 1978), Annex, 6. *See also* Manitoba, Manitoba Housing and Renewal Corporation, *SAFER: Shelter Allowances for Elderly Renters* (Winnipeg: Manitoba Housing and Renewal Corporation, 1981); New Brunswick, *RATE: Rental Assistance to the Elderly* (1978). It may be noted that thinking within the Canada Mortgage and Housing Corporation is very sympathetic to the same formula. *See* the proposed CMHC proposed shelter program analyzed in Derek Hum & Associates, Ltd., *Shelter Allowances and Work Incentives: An Exploratory Assessment* (Ottawa: Canada Mortgage and Housing Corporation, 1981), 2.

8. Forma Consultants, *A Brief Review of the International Experience With Housing Allowances* (Ottawa, 1978), Annex, Table 2.

9. Denmark, Ministry of Housing, *Current Trends and Policies in the Field of Housing, Building and Planning, 1979* (Copenhagen: Ministry of Housing, 1979), 10-11; N. Zeyl, *op. cit.*, 172-75; information supplied by Hanne Victor Hansen, Ministry of Housing, April 23, 1982.

10. Germany, Federal Republic of, Ministry for Land Development, Construction and Urbanization, *Rent Allowance: 1978* (Germantown, MD: HUD USER, 1977). *See also idem., Rent Allowance and Rent Report,* also obtainable from HUD USER.

11. *Idem., Rent Allowance: 1978,* 15.

12. Keijo Tanner, *The Finnish Housing Allowance System for Families and Single Persons as Applied in 1983* (Helsinki: National Housing Board, 1983), 4-11.

13. *Ibid.,* 3.

14. France, Ministere de l'Equipement, *La Reforme du Logement* (December-January 1977), 8-11; Ministere de l'Environement et du Cadre de Vie, *L'Aide Personnalisee au Logement* (Paris: Ministere de l'Equipement, 1978).

15. Hugo Priemus, *Housing Allowances in the Netherlands* (Delft: Delft University Press, 1984), 33-37; 48-56.

16. Norway, Ministry of Local Government and Labour, *Current Trends and Policies in the Field of Housing, Building and Planning* (Oslo: Ministry of Local Government and Labour, 1978), 7-8; *idem.* (Oslo, 1973), 9-10; K. F. Watson, F. Ermuth, and W. Hamilton, *A Comparative Analysis of Housing Allowance Programs* (Ottawa: Central Mortgage and Housing Corporation, 1978), F26-27; N. Zeyl, *op. cit.,* 181-82.

17. Birger Eines, *The Rent Grant System (Rent Allowance)—A Selective Subsidy* (Oslo, 1977, mimeographed), 2-3.

18. Sweden, National Housing Board, *Housing Allowance 1984* (Stockholm: National Housing Board, 1984), 1-2; Notes on *Housing Allowances* supplied by Ian MacArthur, Administrator, International Department, Ministry of Housing and Physical Planning, December 28, 1984; Housing Subsidy Committee, *Housing Subsidies* (Germantown, MD: HUD USER, 1982); Ministry of Housing and Physical Planning, *Human Settlements in Sweden: Current Situation and Related Trends and Policies* (Stockholm: Ministry of Housing and Physical Planning, 1983), 81-82.

19. Gunter Schwerz, *Systems and Significance of Individual Subsidization of Accommodation Costs in European Countries* (Bonn: Domus-Verlag, 1966), 50-54.

20. The rationale behind the 17 percent figure is as follows: It is believed that no more than one-half of the income above the needs allowance should go for taxes and other payments such as rent. Since it is estimated that taxes take one-third of all income above the needs allowance level, this leaves one-sixth of the excess—that is, 17 percent—available for increased rent.

21. Michael John Oxley, "Housing Policy in Western Europe: An Economic Analysis of the Aims and Instruments of Housing Policy in the United Kingdom, West Germany, France, the Netherlands, Denmark and Ireland" (Ph.D. diss., Leicester University, 1983), 283-85; J. B. Cullingworth, *Housing Allowances: The British Experience* (Toronto: Centre for Urban and Community Studies, University of Toronto, 1977), 18-22.

22. Abt Associates, *Participation and Benefits in the Urban Section 8 Program,* 2 vols. (Washington, D.C.: U.S. Department of Housing and Urban Development, 1981).

23. United States, Department of Housing and Urban Development, *News Release* (Washington, D.C., July 30, 1984).

24. Ira S. Lowry, *Experimenting With Housing Allowances* (Cambridge, MA: Oelgeschlager, Gunn and Hain, 1983), 13; Garland E. Allen, Jerry J. Fitts, and Evelyn S. Glatt, "The Experimental Housing Allowance Program" in *Do Housing*

Allowances Work?, eds., Katherine L. Bradbury and Anthony Downs (Washington, D.C.: The Brookings Institution, 1981), 1-32; Marc Benedick, Jr., and Anne D. Squire, "The Three Experiments" in *Housing Vouchers for the Poor*, Raymond J. Struyk and Marc Benedick, Jr. (Washington, D.C.: Urban Institute Press, 1981), Chap. III.
    25. Stephen D. Kennedy and Jean MacMillan, *Participation Under Alternative Housing Allowance Programs: Evidence From the Housing Allowance Demand Experiment* (Cambridge, MA: Abt Associates, 1980), 16-18. Actually a third model, that is, the so-called Unconstrained Model, was tested, but since it was substantially the same as the Housing Gap Model, it is ignored.

7

Where's the Money Coming From?

The principal financial responsibility for housing allowance systems has been assumed by national governments (Table 9). For the most part, the systems have been conceived at the national level and implemented by the national ministry of housing or other equivalent ministry.

In some countries, however, the financial responsibilities are divided between the levels of government. In Denmark there is a 50-50 sharing by the national government with municipalities. In Norway the ratio is 75 percent by the national government and 25 percent by municipalities. The Swedish government finances 100 percent of the cost of the general housing allowance system, 43 percent of the cost of the combined national and municipal plan, and 25 percent of the cost of the supplementary program for pensioners. In Belgium, the Ministry of Public Health and Family Welfare reimburses the National Housing Society for rent remissions which its member societies extend to families with a large number of children. In the Federal Republic of Germany, the states (Lander) finance the allowances and are reimbursed for 50 percent of the cost by the federal government.

When the housing allowance system was established in the United Kingdom in 1972, it envisaged a declining role for the central government. With respect to rent rebates in the public sector, the national government agreed to finance 90 percent of the cost in 1972-73, 85 percent in 1973-74, 80 percent in 1974-75, and 75 percent thereafter. With respect to rent allowances for the private sector, the national government initially assumed complete financial responsibility, on the understanding that the contribution would be progressively reduced in agreement with local authorities. The federal government in Australia shared one program on a 50-50 basis with the states and another program on a 60-40 basis.

In France, the first housing allowance system adopted in 1948 primarily for families suffering hardship as a result of rent increases was financed out of the National Family Allowance Fund and not by the housing ministry. The second housing allowance system for the elderly, the physically handicapped, and young workers was financed by an employer's contribution of 1 percent of wages and by the National Agency for Improvement of the Habitat, which obtains funds from a 3.50 percent surtax on lease fees.[1] The third housing allowance system adopted in 1977 on a more general basis is financed mainly from the housing ministry budget.

In most cases national contributions have come from general tax revenue. However, in Austria, there is a specific earmarking of a portion of the income tax, the corporate tax, and contributions from employers and workers.

In a few countries, provincial and municipal governments have assumed a great amount of responsibility and undertaken their own initiatives. For example, in Canada and Switzerland, provincial, cantonal, and municipal governments established their own plans from their own financial resources without waiting for the national government to take action.

NOTES

1. Raymond Barre (Chairman), *Report of a Commission to Study a Reform of the Financing of Housing* (Germantown, MD: HUD USER, 1984), 27. Translation of the *Rapport de la Commission d'Etude d'une Reforme du Financement du Logement* (Paris: La Documentation Francaise, 1975).

TABLE 9

Financial Sources for Housing Allowances in Highly Industrialized Countries

Country	Percentage by National Government	Percentage by Provincial or State Governments	Percentage by Municipalities	Source of Contribution
Australia				
Rental Rebate (1945)[1]	60	40	0	—
Rental Housing Assistance[2]	50	50	0	—
Pensioner Plan[3]	100	—	—	
Proposed Housing Allowance Plan (1978)[4]	100	0	0	—
Austria[5]	100	0	0	—
Belgium[6]	100	0	0	—
Canada				
Rent Supplement Program[7]	50	50	0	—
Provincial Systems[7]	0	100	0	—
Proposed Federal Plan[8]	100	0	0	—
Denmark[9]				
Pensioner System	75	0	25	—
Nonpensioner System	40	0	60	—
Finland[10]				
General Plan	100	0	0	—
Pensioner Plan	56.5 (Folk Pension Fund)	0	43.5	—
Student Plan	100	0	0	—
France[11]				—

System				Source
Family System (48)	100	0	0	Family Allowance Fund
Social System (71)	100	0	0	National Fund for Housing Assistance—0.1 payroll tax
General System (77)	100	0	0	National Fund general revenue
Germany, Federal Republic of[12]	50	50	0	Federal Government reimburses Lander (states) 50% of outlay
Netherlands, the [13]	100	0	0	—
Norway[14]	75	0	25	—
Sweden[15]				
National System	100	0	0	—
Nat.-Munic. System	43	0	57	—
Supplemental to Pension	75	0	25	—
Switzerland[16]				
Cantonal System (Basle)	0	100	0	—
Municipal System (Zurich)	0	0	100	—
United Kingdom[17]	75	0	25	—
United States[18]	100	0	0	General Tax Revenue

SOURCES

1. Australia: Ministry for Works and Housing, *Homes for Australia* (Canberra, 1949), 5.
2. Australia: Department of Social Security, *Annual Report, 1981–82* (Canberra, 1982), 61.
3. Australia: Information provided by Warwick Temby, Department of Housing and Construction, January 17, 1985.
4. Australia: Department of Environment, Housing and Community Development, *Housing Allowance Experiment: Final Design* (Canberra, 1978), Vol. 1, 1-2.
5. Austria: N. Zeyl, "Systems of Individual Subsidies" in United Nations Economic Commission for Europe, Committee on Housing, Building and Planning, *Financing of Housing* (Geneva, 1973), 163.

SOURCES (Table 9 continued)

6. Belgium: Ministry of Public Health and Family Welfare, *Social Housing Policy in Belgium* (Germantown, MD: HUD USER, 1969), 57, 102.

7. Canada: Canada Mortgage and Housing Corporation.

8. Canada: Canada Mortgage and Housing Corporation, *Some Considerations For Interdepartmental Task Force on Shelter Allowances* (Ottawa, 1981, mimeographed), Sec. 4.3.1.1.

9. Denmark: Information supplied by Hanne Victor Hansen, Denmark, Ministry of Housing, April 23, 1982.

10. Finland: Information provided by Keijo Tanner, National Housing Board, January 12, 1985.

11. France: Ministere de L'Urbanisme et du Logement, *Rapport du Groupe de Travail sur la Reforme Des Aides Personnelles au Logement* (Paris, 1982), 45-46.

12. Germany, Federal Republic of: Ministry for Regional Planning, Building and Urban Development, *Housing, Building and Planning in the Federal Republic of Germany* (Bonn, 1980), 77.

13. Netherlands, the: Hugo Priemus, *Housing Allowances in the Netherlands* (Delft: Delft University Press, 1984), 41-47.

14. Norway: N. Zeyl, "Systems of Individual Subsidies," United Nations Economic Commission for Europe, Committee on Housing, Building and Planning, *Financing of Housing* (Geneva, 1973), 163.

15. Sweden: Ministry of Housing and Physical Planning, *Housing, Building and Planning in Sweden* (Stockholm, 1980), 20. Information provided by Ian MacArthur, Ministry of Housing and Physical Planning, December 28, 1984.

16. Switzerland: Gunter Schwerz, *Systems and Significance of Individual Subsidization of Accommodation Costs in European Countries* (Bonn: Domus-Verlag, 1966), 51-62.

17. United Kingdom: J. B. Cullingworth, *Housing Allowances: The British Experience* (Toronto: Centre for Urban and Community Studies, 1977), 16.

18. United States: Office of Policy Development and Research, *Experimental Housing Allowance Program* (Washington, D.C.: U.S. Department of Housing and Urban Development, 1980), xxiv.

8

Housing Allowances and National Housing Subsidy Policy: An Overview

Highly industrialized countries have now had two to three decades of experience with housing allowances. What does the overall picture look like?

Unfortunately the information available at the international level on the performance of housing allowance programs is incomplete. Table 10 presents the most recent available data on participants and payments in housing allowance systems.

Two major conclusions emerge. First, in four countries (Finland, France, Sweden, and the United Kingdom), approximately one-fifth or more—and in three additional countries (Australia, Denmark, and the Netherlands) approximately one-tenth or more—of total households are recipients of some form of housing allowance. Since 1980 census household data are not yet generally available, 1970 data were used. Therefore, these fractions are only approximations. This testifies to the considerable importance which the housing allowance has assumed in the everyday life of highly industrialized countries.

Second, average housing allowance payments in most countries amount to $500 or more per year, that is, around $42 or more per month. This is a substantial contribution to the family budget and to a reduction of the rent burden on low-income families.

Turning to subsidy policy as a whole, what is the relative importance of housing allowances in national housing subsidy expenditures? Available

TABLE 10
Housing Allowance Participants and Payments in Highly Industrialized Countries

Country	Households		Housing Allowance Participants as % of Total	Total Housing Allowance Payments (000,000)		Average Annual Household Housing Allowance	
	Total[1] (1970–71 Census) (000)	No. of Housing Allowance Participants (000)		US $[2]	Local Currency	US $[2]	Local Currency
Australia	3,672	[555](82)*	15	287	A$ 282(82)	517	A$ 508(82)
Pensioner Plan[3]	—	417(82)	—	157	A$ 160(82)	376	A$ 383(82)
Public Hous. Plan[4]	—	138(82)	—	120	A$ 122(82)	869	A$ 884(82)
Austria[5]	2,536	—	—	41	A$ 589(78)	—	—
Belgium[6]	3,234	—	—		BF 1,424(79)	—	—
Canada							
Nat'l Hsg. Act Rent Supplement[7]	8,281[7]	21(84)	0.25	41	C$ 54(84)	1,957	C$ 2,571(84)
British Columbia[8]	—	14.7(78)	—	8	C$ 9(78)	515	C$ 588(78)
Denmark[9]	1,850	[239](82)	13	228	DK 1,902(82)	955	DK 7,958(82)
Pensioner Plan	—	169(82)	—		DK 1,395(82)	991	DK 8,254(82)
Nonpens. Plan	—	70(82)	—		DK 507(82)	869	DK 7,243(82)
Finland[10]	1,781(80)[10]	[357](83)	20	216	FM 1,206(83)	606	FM 3,378(83)
Pensioner Plan	—	179(83)	—	83	FM 460(83)	461	FM 2,570(83)
General Plan	—	102(83)	—	104	FM 579(83)	1,019	FM 5,676(83)
Student Plan	—	76(83)	—	30	FM 167(83)	394	FM 2,197(83)
France[11]	15,778	[3,190](81)	20	2,498	FF 13,573(81)[12]	783	FF 4,255(81)
Family Plan	—	1,920(81)	—	1,525	FF 8,286(81)	794	FF 4,315(81)
Social Plan	—	915(81)	—	630	FF 3,424(81)	689	FF 3,742(81)
Personal Plan	—	355(81)	—	343	FF 1,863(81)	966	FF 5,248(81)
Germany, Fed. Rep.[12]	21,991	1,820(82)	8	1,099	DM 2,667(82)	604	DM 1,465(82)
Ireland[13]	731	Real avg. public hsg. rents declined 32% from 1972 to 1977 (Differential Rent Program)					
Netherlands, the[14]	3,990	444(81)	11	248	FL 620(81)	559	FL 1,396(81)
Norway[15]	1,297	107(77)	8	44	NK 235(77)	413	NK 2,196(77)
	—	—	—	72	NK 383(79)[16]	—	—

Sweden[17]	3,050	[1,200](81)	39	1,185	SK 6,000(81)	987	SK 5,000(81)
National Plan	—	400(81)	—	—	—	—	—
Munic. Pen. Plan	—	800(81)	—	—	—	—	—
United Kingdom[18]	18,623	[3,700](79)	20	[2,389]	£ 1,126(79-80)	—	£ 304(79-80)
Suppl. Benefit	—	2,300(79)	—	1,837	£ 866(79-80)	819	£ 386(79-80)
Rent Rebate-pub.	—	1,200(79)	—	471	£ 222(79-80)	392	£ 185(79-80)
Rent Allow.-priv.	—	200(79)	—	81	£ 38(79-80)	369	£ 174(79-80)
United States[19]							
Section 8 Prog.	80,000(80)	1,958(84)	24	—	$ 5,811(84)	—	$ 2,967(84)

*The numbers in parentheses refer to relevant year.

SOURCES

1. United Nations Economic Commission for Europe, Committee on Housing, Building and Planning, *Housing Situation in the ECE Countries Around 1970* (New York, 1978), Table 1. Australia 1971 data from United Nations, *Compendium of Housing Statistics, 1972–74* (New York, 1976), 63.
2. Local currency prices converted at the then-existing exchange rate. International Monetary Fund, *International Financial Statistics Yearbook 1983* (Washington, D.C., 1984).
3. Australia: Tim Field, "Pensioners Who Rent—Problems and Alternatives," *Social Security Journal* (Canberra, June 1983), 25.
4. *Ibid.* 26.
5. Austria: Federal Ministry of Construction and Technology, *Current Trends and Policies in the Field of Housing, Building and Planning* (Vienna, 1980), 16.
6. Belgium: Institut National de Statistique, *Statistiques de la Construction et du Logement* (Brussels, 1981), 195. See also Ministry of Public Health and Family Welfare, *Social Housing Policy in Belgium* (Germantown, MD: HUD USER, 1969), 102, 108.
7. Canada: Canada Mortgage and Housing Corporation estimates, information provided by Frances Cameron, Director, Planning Division, February 12, 1985.
8. Canada: British Columbia, Ministry of Municipal Affairs and Housing, *Profile of the SAFER Beneficiaries* (Vancouver, 1978), 2, 12.
9. Denmark: Ministry of Housing, *Financing of Housing Subsidies in Denmark* (Paper prepared for United Nations Economic Commission for Europe, Committee on Housing, Building and Planning, Seminar on Housing, April 24, 1984), 35-36.
10. Finland: Keijo Tanner, *The Finnish Housing Allowance System for Families and Single Persons as Applied in 1983* (Helsinki: National Housing Board, 1983), App. 10.
11. France: Ministry of Urban Planning and Housing, Jacques Badet (Chairman), *Report of the Working Group on the Reform of Personal Housing Assistance* (Germantown, MD: HUD USER, 1982), 35.
12. Germany, Federal Republic of: Ministry for Regional Planning, Housing and Municipal Planning, *Housing Allowance and Rent: 1983 Report* (Germantown, MD: HUD USER, 1984), 16.
13. Ireland: National Institute for Physical Planning and Construction Research, *Public Subventions to Housing in Ireland* (Dublin, 1978), 29.

SOURCES (Table 10 continued)

14. Netherlands, the: Ministry of Housing, Physical Planning and Environment, *Some Data on House-Building in the Netherlands* (Hague, 1983), 37-39. The number of households rose to 5,071,000 in 1983 [Ministerie van Volkshuisvesting, Ruimtelijke Ordening en Milieubeheer (Hague, 1984), Tables 14 and 18], and the number of participants rose to an estimated 750,000 in 1984. Cited in Hugo Priemus, *Housing Allowances in the Netherlands* (Delft: Delft University Press, 1984), 71.

15. Norway: Ministry of Local Government and Labour, *Current Trends and Policies in the Field of Housing, Building and Planning* (Oslo, 1978), 8.

16. *Idem., Current Trends and Policies in the Field of Human Settlements* (Oslo, 1980), 20.

17. Sweden: Ministry of Housing and Physical Planning, *Human Settlements in Sweden* (Stockholm, 1983), 76, 82.

18. United Kingdom: Department of the Environment, *Assistance With Housing Costs* (London, 1981, mimeographed), Annex A.

19. United States: Office of Policy Development and Research, *1982 National Housing Production Report* (Washington, D.C.: U.S. Department of Housing and Urban Development, 1983), App. B, 9; *ibid., Housing Payments* (work sheets).

data are even more unsatisfactory on the larger subsidy issues than on housing allowance systems *per se*. Few continuous time series are available, definitions are not always comparable, and there is undoubtedly an underreporting of many forms of indirect housing subsidies, particularly those granted by provincial and municipal governments. This means that the percentages, which have been calculated in Table 11 concerning the role of housing allowances in total national housing subsidies, are in all probability overestimates. Nevertheless, recognizing their weaknesses and limited value, two general conclusions can be drawn.

First, in seven countries (Australia, Denmark, Finland, France, the Netherlands, Sweden, and the United Kingdom), housing allowances constitute roughly one-quarter or more of the total national housing subsidies. This is an impressive figure.

Second, if tax subsidies (mainly in the form of tax deductibility of mortgage interest payments) are excluded, then the relative importance of housing allowances is considerably increased. In five countries (Finland, France, the Netherlands, Sweden, and the United Kingdom), they account for one-third to one-half of the total housing subsidies.

TABLE 11
Composition of Housing Subsidies in Highly Industrialized Countries*

Country	Housing Allowances and Rent Rebates (000,000)	Producer Subsidies (000,000)	Tax Concessions (000,000)	Other Subsidies (000,000)	Total Housing Subsidies (000,000)	Housing Allowances As % of Subsidies	
						Total	Total Excl. Tax Sub.
Australia[1]	A$ 242(83)	A$ 623(83)	None	A$ 265(83)	A$ 1,130(83)	21	21
Austria[2]	AS 589(78)	AS 3,152(78) New AS 1,079(78) Reh.	—	—	AS 4,820(78)	12	—
Belgium[3]	BF 1,424(79)	BF10,249(79)	—	BF 752(79)	BF12,425(79)	11	—
Canada[4]	C$ 27(84)	C$ 990(84)	C$ 300(84)	C$ 240(84)	C$ 1,557(84)	0.2	0.2
Denmark[5]	DK 3,000(84)	DK 3,540(84)	DK 3,500(84)	—	DK10,040(84)	30	46
Finland[6]	FM 961(81)	FM 1,400(81)	FM 1,050(81)	—	FM 3,411(81)	28	41
France	FF12,433(84)[7]	FF19,741(84)[7]	FF24,500(82)[8]	—	FF56,674(82-84)(?)	22(?)	39(?)
Germany, Fed. Republic of[9]	DM 1,900(78)	DM 4,700(78)	DM10,950(78)	DM 4,450(78)	DM22,000(78)	9	27
Ireland[10]	—	£150(77)	—	—	—	—	—
Netherlands, the[11]	FL 1,800(83)	FL 2,300(83)	FL1,850(75)[12]	FL 800(83)	FL 6,750(75-83)(?)	27(?)	37(?)
Norway[13]	NK 383(79)	—	—	—	—	—	—
Sweden[14]	SK 6,000(81)	SK 7,200(81)	SK 11,500(81)	—	SK24,700(81)	24	45
United Kingdom	B£11,126(75-6)[15]	B£1,066(75-6)[16]	B£ 1,450(79-80)[17]	—	B£3,642(75-80)(?)	31(?)	—
United States[18]	$ 3,115(81)	$ 2,351(81)	$34,500(81)	$1,205(81)	$41,071(81)	7.6	46.7

*Warning: Calculations for France, the Netherlands, and the United Kingdom based on data for different years. The numbers in parentheses refer to relevant year.

SOURCES

1. Australia: Information provided by Warwick Temby, Department of Housing and Construction, January 17, 1985. In 1984-85 federal subsidies were as follows: pensioner plan—$242 million; public housing—$623 million; assistance to first homebuyer—$265 million. In addition, there were housing loans to veterans of $129 million. *See also* Minister of Finance, *Budget Statements: 1983-4* (Canberra, 1983), Budget Paper No. 1, 141-45.

2. Austria: Federal Ministry of Construction and Technology, *Current Trends and Policies in the Field of Housing, Building and Planning* (Vienna, 1980), 16.

3. Belgium: Institut National de Statistique, *Statistiques de la Construction et du Logement* (Brussels, 1981), 195.

4. Canada: Information provided by Frances Cameron, Director, Planning Division, Canada Mortgage and Housing Corporation, February 12, 1985. In addition, provincial governments financed directly the following subsidies: shelter allowances—C$417 million; producer subsidies—C$49 million; tax concessions—C$491 million; and other subsidies—C$96 million.

5. Denmark: Ministry of Housing, *Financing of Housing and Housing Subsidies in Denmark* (Paper presented to United Nations Economic Commission for Europe, Committee on Housing, Building and Planning, Seminar on Housing, April 24, 1984), 19-20.

6. Finland: Ministry of Interior and National Housing Board, *Monograph on the Human Settlements Situation and Related Trends and Policies* (Helsinki, 1982), 45-46.

7. France: Ministere de L'Urbanisme et du Logement, *Repartition des Aides de l'Etat au Logement Par Nature de Financement* (Paris, 1984), 2.

8. France: Ministere de L'Urbanisme et du Logement, *Rapport du Groupe de Travail sur la Reforme des Aides Personnelles au Logement* (Paris, 1982), 35.

9. Germany, Federal Republic of: German Marshall Fund of the United States, *US/British/German Discussion of Housing Policy* (Washington, D.C., 1979, mimeographed), 16.

10. Ireland: National Institute for Physical Planning and Construction Research, *Public Subventions to Housing in Ireland* (Dublin, 1978), 59.

11. Netherlands, the: Hugo Priemus, *Housing Allowances in the Netherlands* (Delft: Delft University Press, 1984), 45. Total housing subsidies are the total budgeted expenses for housing and physical planning.

12. Netherlands, the: Organisation for Economic Cooperation and Development, *Tax Expenditures and Home Ownership* (Paris, 1977), 16A.

13. Norway: Ministry of Local Government and Labour, *Current Trends and Policies in the Field of Human Settlements* (Oslo, 1980), 20.

14. Sweden: Ministry of Housing and Physical Planning, *Human Settlements in Sweden* (Stockholm, 1983), 76.

15. United Kingdom: Department of the Environment, *Assistance with Housing Costs* (London, 1981, mimeographed). Annex A.

16. United Kingdom: *Ibid. Housing Policy, Technical Volume* (London, H.M.S.O., 1977), Pt. II, 19.

17. United Kingdom: David Donnison, "A Rationalization of Housing Benefits," *Three Banks' Review* (September 1981), 8.

18. United States: Office of Policy Development and Research, *1982 National Housing Production Report* (Washington, D.C.: U.S. Department of Housing and Urban Development, 1983), App. A, 2; *Idem, Housing Payments* (work sheets).

Assessment and Conclusions

9

Impact of Housing Allowances

The first step in assessing housing allowances is to examine their impact in terms of realizing their original objectives and those of housing subsidy policies in general. This chapter will, therefore, measure their impact against two general criteria: the degree to which they have improved physical living conditions; and the degree to which they have reduced excessive rent burdens. It will then review the degree of success achieved by the eight different housing allowance strategies analyzed in Chapter 2. Finally, it will examine the impact on public housing.

The second step is to weigh the relative advantages and disadvantages of the consumer subsidy approach with those of the producer subsidy approach—one of the central issues in housing policy today. This is done in Chapter 10.

The third step is to analyze the housing allowance concept as opposed to the more generalized income maintenance approach, which has been increasingly discussed in recent years. This is taken up in Chapter 11.

Finally, there is a summing up on housing allowance systems in Chapter 12.

Physical Living Conditions

Undoubtedly the dominant objective of governments in housing subsidy policy is to ensure that all families live in decent housing. This objective is accomplished in two ways: by constructing new housing; and by rehabilitating and modernizing existing housing. How effective have housing allowances been in improving physical living conditions? The record on this score is mixed. One of the major purposes of the German housing allowance system adopted in 1965, apparently, was to bring housing finance more into line with the principles of the country's socially oriented, free-market economy and, thus, to stimulate construction of new housing. Similarly in Sweden, *inter alia*, housing allowances were designed to improve the housing supply, and in Austria they were expected to stimulate indirectly the construction of new housing.[1] One of the main goals of the United States Experimental Housing Program (EHAP) was to induce low-income households to live in better housing.

As observed in Chapter 4, Physical Structure, a majority of European housing allowance plans require that participants live in minimum standard dwellings, and some sort of housing inspection system is normally applied. For the majority of housing allowance recipients already living in minimum standard housing, the subsidy system plays a useful—albeit passive—role in support of good living conditions. As regards households living in substandard housing, housing allowances have played a more active role. Assuming that the renter does not want to forego the allowance, either the owner has to bring the dwelling up to standard so that the renter can receive the allowance; or the renter has to seek standard accommodations elsewhere. As a matter of fact, in many countries, such as Denmark, the Federal Republic of Germany, Sweden, and the United Kingdom, rent increases accompanying housing allowances have been permitted on the condition that the landlord spend at least part of the increased income on maintenance and repair to bring the dwelling unit up to standard. In these ways the housing allowance has in the short-run indirectly stimulated an improvement in housing conditions.

In the United States, about half of those enrolled in the EHAP supply experiment lived in dwellings that did not meet minimum standards. Among those who had to upgrade the quality of their accommodation to qualify, about two-thirds did. Thus participation in the program increased the likelihood of occupying standard housing from about 50 to 80 percent. In addition to making required repairs (the average cost of which was about $100), three-fourths of the owners voluntarily improved dwellings each year, and two-fifths of the renters moved to larger or better dwellings. However, the average participant increased housing expenditures by only 8 percent over what they would otherwise have been.[2]

On the other hand, some countries, notably the Federal Republic of Germany, Finland, the Netherlands, Sweden, and the United Kingdom, have not made minimum housing standards a condition of payment, or they have abandoned this condition. In these cases, the housing allowance has not been an active force for improving existing housing conditions.

The long-term impact of housing allowances on the supply of housing is dependent on many variables, such as the degree of initiative and flexibility in the building industry, the quality and capacity of housing finance institutions, the venturesomeness of private capital, the completion of planning required for urban growth, the availability of developed land, and rent controls. On the whole, there is undoubtedly less elasticity in the supply side of the European building industry than in that of the United States. The size and vitality of the private rental housing sector in most European countries have been substantially reduced as a consequence of rent controls during the last four decades.[3] If the vacancy rate is high, the increased demand for decent housing may be met merely by a reduction in the vacancy ratio. The social housing sector, which constitutes a larger share of national housing construction in most European countries than in the United States, does not depend on rising prices as a stimulus to higher production. Moreover, in Europe in general, private land and housing development cannot proceed apace in a spontaneous and uncontrolled manner.

In nonurban areas there may be special problems. For example, in some small communities in Ontario, Canada, there is little or no rental accommmodation and no market potential for private rental development. In these circumstances a houing allowance program has little or no effect in increasing the supply of housing; a new subsidized rental or home ownership program may be the only way to add standard housing to the existing housing stock. Similarly with regard to special housing needs, for example, the physically handicapped, a housing allowance program may have limited capacity to create new housing with the necessary special design features.

The favorable impact of the housing allowance on physical living conditions tends to be confirmed by a few fragmentary studies. In the Federal Republic of Germany during the period 1974-76, the size of dwellings (rental and owner-occupied) of housing allowance recipients increased less than 2 percent, while rents increased 15 to 17 percent. Since rents for dwellings with comparable facilities did not increase substantially, the government concluded that there had been an improvement in housing quality.[4]

Hugo Priemus points out that one-half of the occupants of new rental housing in the Netherlands receive a housing allowance. Since the high rate of new housing construction could not be maintained without the demand support provided by the consumer housing subsidy, he concludes that the system clearly had a stimulating effect on new construction and renovation.[5]

In Canada the probable impact of the housing allowance system on housing consumption in six major cities was examined in a simulation study for the Canada Mortgage and Housing Corporation: Would households use the assistance to increase housing consumption, or would it be used for the purchase of other goods and services? The study found that over a future 10-year period a surprisingly high 70 percent of participants would likely increase the quality of their housing consumption.[6]

On the other hand, a contrary view of Canadian experience was reached by Marion Steele. She finds that there has not been a substantial housing consumption response from housing allowance recipients. Even if in the long-run there were such a response, she contends that it would be only partly in the form of increased physical quality because low-income households appear to spend an increase in income as much to reduce crowding as to increase housing quality.[7]

Furthermore, she suggests one reason why low-income households seemingly spend so little of any increased income on housing may be that they are already spending more than they would freely choose to spend in an unregulated market. Building code regulations dictate that in most cases they must occupy and pay for well-built accommodations with complete basic facilities. The quite high incidence of primitive toilet and other facilities in rural areas among low-income households may be regarded as presumptive evidence that many low-income urban households might prefer to spend their money on more and better food, clothing, and other goods and services rather than on well-built and serviced housing.[8]

In summary, the role of housing allowances in improving physical living conditions appears to have been considerable, although relatively indirect. It is probably true to say that the great majority of those receiving housing allowances already live in minimum standard housing. In the short-run, the housing allowance has been a positive factor in promoting rehabilitation of some substandard dwelling units.

In the long-run, the increased demand for minimum housing generated by housing allowance systems has undoubtedly helped to stimulate new housing construction and to stabilize the level of housing construction. It is reasonable to assume that if funds are placed in the hands of low-income families sufficient to enable them to pay the full economic rent of decent housing, then in the long-run and in principle the market mechanism will respond and ultimately provide the quantity of new housing required to meet the demand. This will be particularly true for young households who are "first timers" on the housing market.

Rent Burden

A second major concern in national housing subsidy policy is to reduce, if not eliminate, the excessive rent burden which poor families bear. The success of the housing allowance in accomplishing this purpose depends on several factors: the level of individual subsidies; the comprehensiveness of coverage; the rate of enrollment; any offsetting rent increases; and the degree of flexibility in eligible income ceilings.

First, the introduction of housing allowances has certainly had a significant impact on rent burdens carried by low-income and moderate-income families.[9] Tables 2 and 3 provide general information on shelter-to-income ratios. Additional detailed data are available for several countries. In Finland, in 1982, housing allowances reduced the cost of shelter for renters from 27.8 percent of disposable income to 14.3 percent, and for owners from 21.9 to 13 percent.[10] The 1977 French housing allowance program reduced the shelter-to-income ratio (including within rent the French concept, "charges," that is loosely translated, utilities) from 22.9 percent under the old system to 18.8 percent under the reformed system.[11]

In the Federal Republic of Germany housing allowances account for one-third of recipients' total rent payments, reducing the ratio of housing cost to gross income by 6 to 9 percent, depending on the level of household income.[12] In the 1978 British Columbia Shelter Aid to Elderly Renters Program (Canada), the amount of personal income spent on rent was reduced from an average of 47 percent to 34 percent.[13] While the 34 percent reflected substantial improvement, it was still above the 25 percent which the national government established as the SIR ratio ceiling in its public housing program (Table 3). The Dutch housing allowance system in 1980-81 reduced the average SIR ratio of 20.4 percent for recipients before subsidization to 15.6 percent after subsidization.[14] In the South Australian Mortgage and Rent Relief Plan, before receiving assistance, 72 percent of the recipients were paying more than 40 percent of their incomes in rent; after receiving rent relief only 8 percent of participants were so burdened.[15]

In the United States, the Experimental Housing Allowance Program in the supply demonstration projects lowered the average SIR from 50 percent of gross income to 30 percent. Although allowances augmented the typical renter's income of $4,100 by about a fourth and the typical owner's income of $4,600 by a sixth, they chose to spend only a fifth of the extra money on housing. Thus, four-fifths of all allowance payments were allocated to nonhousing consumption.[16]

The extent of coverage is a second factor in measuring the impact on rent burdens: the more restricted the coverage, obviously the more limited the impact; conversely, the more general the coverage, the greater the potential impact. As seen in Chapter 2, the earliest housing allowance systems were highly restrictive, being targeted toward the neediest groups in the population: large families and the elderly. Within the last decade, however, the trend has been clearly toward opening up the housing allowance to all low-income households. The percentage of households receiving a housing allowance is fairly impressive (Table 10). Sweden has the broadest coverage, with roughly 39 percent of the households receiving some form of housing allowance. In Finland, France, and the United Kingdom, it is approximately one-fifth or more, while in Australia, Denmark, and the Netherlands, it is approximately one-tenth or over.

Third, there has been a disinterest and an unwillingness on the part of many low-income families to participate in the system. As observed in Chapter 5, Enrollment, the enrollment rate has been low in the private rental housing sector in many countries. A major obstacle seems to be the "means test." Finding the test demeaning, many families prefer to forego their rights rather than submit their private financial affairs to public scrutiny. In addition, some families, particularly the elderly, may not be aware of their options, in spite of efforts to publicize the availability of the allowance. For other families, the amount of the benefit has been so small and so subject to change that it may not be worth bothering about. In the Netherlands, for example, most private rental dwellings are old, low-standard, low-rent accommodations; when rents are low, there is much less need for housing allowances. In still other cases, families prefer to remain in their existing accommodation, even though it may be substandard, rather than search for and move to alternative housing that meets current housing standards. A way has to be devised for enrolling all needy families in the housing allowance system.

A fourth important factor is: To what extent have landlords undermined the value of allowances by raising rents? Dennis and Fish, in their analysis of the housing allowance concept for the Canada Mortgage and Housing Corporation, observe that the traditional weakness of the housing allowance is leakage, that is, "the proposed transfers will leak out of the hands of recipients into the pockets of their landlords."[17] For example, if a housing allowance is designed to reduce the shelter-to-income ratio from 35 to 25 percent, but if meanwhile the landlord has increased the rent by an equivalent amount, then the excessive rent burden remains unchanged.

Actual market behavior on this issue is mixed. Perhaps the major factor is the elasticity of the housing supply. Traditionally, housing supply has been regarded as relatively inelastic, particularly in the short run. A great amount of lead time is required to undertake land development, obtain approval of house plans, arrange financing, complete construction, and deliver new housing for occupancy. But experience has demonstrated considerable short-term elasticity in many cases.

One crucial variable is the vacancy rate; the size of rent increases tends to vary inversely with the vacancy rates.[18] The higher the vacancy rate, the greater will be the force of competition among landlords tending to hold down rent increases and less the likelihood of rent increases that will absorb a part of any housing allowance. Conversely, the lower the vacancy rate, the greater the possibility that rents will be increased to capture a part of the housing allowance. In Canadian deliberations on this issue, it has been pointed out that it would be difficult to prevent leakages in two subsectors of the national housing market where the housing supply is limited: that is, in most rural communities where an adequate private rental housing market does not generally exist; and in housing for groups with special needs, such as the physically handicapped.[19]

Another factor affecting leakages is the size of the housing allowance and the number of recipients at the time the system is introduced in a given geographic area. If the size and the number are relatively small, the impact will clearly be much less than if they are large.

Rent control is another important variable. If there is no rent control in a given private rental housing market, then there may be considerable risk of leakage, particularly if the vacancy rate is low and if there are a large number of participants. But if rent regulations are in force, as they continue to be in some form in most European countries, an anticipatory rent increase is rather unlikely if as a national policy the purpose of the housing allowance is to lower the heavy rent burden. The International Federation for Housing and Planning has recommended that rent control be used as a tool to prevent rent inflation from accompanying the introduction of housing allowances.[20]

The housing allowance might have still another possible long-term market effect of a favorable character. Nonpayment of rent and high turnover associated with fluctuating household incomes of low-income families are major costs for private landlords. By introducing a stabilizing flow of income, the housing allowance tends to reduce these costs to landlords and to counterbalance tendencies toward higher rents.[21]

There is little evidence that landlords have profited from the introduction of housing allowance systems by raising rents. European experience on this point may not, however, be an altogether relevant guide for the probable impact of a housing allowance system in the American housing market for two major reasons. First, rent regulations in a majority of large European cities, while often allowing for "fair rent" increases, have placed limits on possible rent increases in the private rental housing sector. There is no way of knowing, therefore, what the impact of housing allowances would have been if European rental housing markets had been free of controls. In the United States, the rental market generally has not been regulated.

Second, inordinate rent increases would be practically inconceivable in the large public housing sector (including the nonprofit housing organization sector) of most countries where rent levels are determined by public authorities. Postwar rent increases in public housing, of which there have been many in most countries, have in general been introduced with overall national considerations in mind: for example, to keep proper adjustment with other general increases in prices and incomes. A leakage would certainly not have been designed to the detriment of the low-income renter. By comparison, the United States has a public sector from one-tenth to one-twentieth the size of that in most highly industrialized European countries.

Market behavior under Canadian provincial housing allowance systems confirms European experience. For example, using the well-known Urban Institute Market Simulation Model (U.S.), Clayton and Associates predicted in 1981 a long-run increase in the price of housing services in Winnipeg, Manitoba, of 33.7 percent. After a year and a half, there was, in fact, a slight decrease rather than an increase. Similar results were found in Vancouver, British Columbia. The primary reason for this seems to have been the low consumption response; that is, recipients may be even less likely to move (and so increase their housing consumption) when the market is very tight than when it is very loose, perhaps because of high search and moving costs in a tight market. Steele concludes that "The possibility of a substantial increase in price in the short-run, even in tight markets, seems remote."[22] She continues by suggesting that there might well be a decline in the long-run price of housing. Housing allowance recipients would be more likely to pay their rent and less likely to move, thus leading in a competitive market to a decline in landlords' turnover costs and bad debts.[23] Australian experience reveals comparatively little inflationary impact as well. During the first 12 months of the Mortgage and Rent Relief Plan in South Australia, only 10 percent of housing allowance recipients reported rent increases.[24]

In 1981 the Canada Mortgage and Housing Corporation undertook a study, *inter alia,* of the question: Do shelter allowances serve only to increase rents? In a simulation study over a 10-year period in six major Canadian cities, using the Urban Institute Market Simulation Model, it was found that the likely average price inflation in the overall housing market would be about 4 percent. The rate varied widely among cities, ranging from 8.4 percent in Winnipeg to 2.6 percent in Calgary to 1.5 percent in Saskatoon. The main reason for these differences was the gap between prevailing rents and the rent required to profitably construct and operate new rental units. For housing allowance participants, the study showed that likely average rent inflation would be at the much higher rate of 15.9 percent.[25]

In the United States, contrary to widespread predictions that EHAP would result in rent increases of 10 percent or more, the maximum increase in the most active submarkets was 2.5 to 3.5 percent. In retrospect, fears of inflationary rents seem to have been based on four misconceptions: (1) that once a household becomes poor, it stays poor, so that virtually all eligible households would participate in a housing allowance program; (2) that all poor households live in substandard housing; (3) that once a dwelling becomes substandard, it stays substandard; and (4) that the short-run supply of housing is inelastic.[26] As a matter of fact, rent increases were less than increases in the costs of operating rental property.

One important factor limiting rent increases in the United States EHAP was the built-in incentive for rent bargaining. The housing allowance paid was the difference between not the factual market rent but the Fair Market Rent—as determined administratively by the Department of Housing and Urban Development—and 25 percent of the adjusted household income. The recipient, therefore, had an incentive to search and bargain for the lowest possible rent for minimum standard housing. If the actual rent paid was less than the Fair Market Rent, then the participant received, in effect, a bonus. Under another similar U.S. housing allowance program—the so-called Section 8 Existing Program—the recipient did not receive any benefit if the actual rent was less than the Fair Market Rent. Without the incentive for searching and bargaining, the rate of rent increase in the Section 8 Existing Program was considerably higher than the rate of rent increase under EHAP. For this reason the administration has proposed to revise the Section 8 Existing Program payment formula along the lines of EHAP and thus encourage participants to shop around for standard housing with the lowest rents.[27]

In most countries housing allowance systems encountered another related price problem. Every inflationary rise in money incomes carries a certain percentage of participants above the ceiling, resulting in their automatic disqualification, although in real terms they are no better off than before. At least three countries, France, the Federal Republic of Germany, and the Netherlands, abandoned fixed income ceilings and introduced a continuous watch on wage developments so as to enable authorities to raise income ceilings whenever necessary.[28] On the other hand, too much flexibility can also be a problem. The adjustment of rent ceilings must be done in such a way as not to become a factor contributing to further inflation in the rental market. One danger is that landlords may see flexibility in rent ceilings as leverage for charging higher rents and thus independently further fueling inflation.

There remains to be discussed a specific accomplice role that the housing allowance system has played in some countries in helping to meet the national objective of harmonizing the rent structure. As described in

Chapter 2, Rent Harmonization Model, one housing subsidy strategy has been to increase low rents on old properties so as to be more in line with higher rents on new properties which have been built at a much higher cost level; and, in the process, this provides landlords with income for maintenance and repairs to reverse the alarming rate of deterioration in the national housing stock. The housing allowance thus became an anticipatory measure to shield low-income households that might suffer hardship from rent increases. To help ensure that all income from increased rents was not creamed off by landlords, some governments, such as Denmark, the Federal Republic of Germany, Sweden, and the United Kingdom, made rent increases conditional on at least part of the income being devoted to needed maintenance and repairs. In such a context, instead of being totally evil, some "leakage" was elevated to high purpose in national policy!

Summarizing, the housing allowance system has been highly successful in converting excessive SIRs into a much more reasonable charge on the average family budget. Moreover, the housing allowance system has been effective in targeting assistance to special areas of need in the housing market, notably the elderly and large families. These achievements, however, are only averages. There are still individual families carrying excessively high rent burdens because of living in new high-cost construction. Foreign experience confirms the findings of the United States Experimental Housing Allowance Program—housing allowances have had comparatively little effect on the price of housing services.

Housing Allowance Strategies

Chapter 2 distinguished eight major strategies which have inspired governments in designing their housing allowance programs. In retrospect, how effective have these strategies been?

In general terms, most strategies have been reasonably successful in accomplishing their purposes.

The large family hardship model and the elderly hardship model dominated the early development of housing allowance policy. Uncontestably, the large family and the elderly represented the two most needy household categories in the population. While there has been a clear tendency within the last decade to broaden the coverage of housing allowance systems to include all low-income households, the principles governing most systems continue to give priority to large families and the elderly. The impact in these respects has been notable.

The rent harmonization model, the third model, reached its zenith in the late 1960s and was most conspicuous in two countries, Denmark and the Netherlands. The strategy was well conceived. As rent controls were relaxed and rents on old housing were permitted to move toward higher market levels, allowances would protect households on fixed incomes from resulting hardship. In this way an equalization of rents would be achieved, producing an overall more efficient housing market. While the housing allowance part of the strategy worked well, expectations of relative stability in new construction costs did not materialize. The cost of new housing rose more rapidly than rents were being increased, with the result that rent differentials tended to remain as wide as ever. Nevertheless, under such a policy, the housing market ended up in much better shape than it would have been in the absence of this policy.

The excessive shelter-to-income model has permeated most thinking about housing allowances. As a generalized conception, it seems to have emerged most clearly in the early 1970s. The impact of housing allowances on SIRs has been dealt with in the preceding section.

The tandem–new construction model became most popular in the early and middle 1970s, when governments were suddenly confronted with rising vacancy rates in new social housing. Rents on the new housing became prohibitive for low-income and middle-income households because of the inflationary rise in housing costs attributable mainly to rapidly increasing land prices and mortgage interest rates. The strategy appears to have made a useful contribution to solving this cost problem.

The social stability model was an ancillary concept entering in some measure in most housing allowance systems. While it is difficult to identify any particular achievements of this strategy, it can be described as generally successful.

The labor mobility model has perhaps been the least successful strategy in application. Partly this is because of divided sentiments about the importance of labor mobility (particularly when it involves trying to get families to move who do not want to move), but perhaps mainly because mobility is a dynamic of the labor market that can be adequately dealt with only by a national active manpower policy. The role of housing allowances is of necessity minor. Nevertheless, some evidence is available on the effect of Dutch allowances on labor mobility. In a sample survey of Dutch housing allowance recipients living in "older housing," 10 percent said they would not have moved into their current accommodation if they had not been eligible for a subsidy; for recipients in "newer" housing, the proportion was 20 percent.[29]

Little information is available on the workings of the family crisis model. But the closely related Australian Mortgage and Rent Relief Scheme appears to have been reasonably successful. One-third of all recipients were single persons. The high mobility and transient nature of many singles keep them in a constant state of change. The program has, therefore, provided effective short-term rent relief for many persons not normally accommodated by public housing. Moreover, the program has substantially lowered shelter-to-income ratios without leading to rent inflation (see Rent Burden above).[30]

Public Housing

In at least one country, Canada, one objective of housing allowance systems has been to reduce the segregation of low-income families in large projects (which sometimes have become ghettos of the poor) and to integrate them into the community at large. Providing allowances to low-income families makes it possible for them—at least theoretically—to go into the market and find housing of their own choice. This tends to promote a more diversified and harmonious society.[31]

It has been suggested that a large-scale, untied housing allowance introduces a threat to the public housing sector. That is to say, if households are given purchasing power to go into the market and find housing of their choice, and if the private sector offers attractive housing alternatives in price, variety, and location, then public housing tenants may be strongly tempted to forsake their existing homes for something better. If, as a consequence, large numbers of tenants do leave public housing, then local housing authorities could be confronted with rising vacancy rates, substantial cost increases, and a general questioning of the continued value of the public housing program.

I 1 European experience there is little evidence that housing allowance systems have adversely affected the public housing sector. Indeed, one of the purposes behind the housing allowance in many countries has been to support public housing by helping to bridge the gap between the high rents on new high-cost housing and the capacity to pay of low-income and moderate-income families. On the other hand, it is not unreasonable to find that, as in the Netherlands, the introduction of a housing allowance increased the vacancy rates in those parts of the existing housing stock that were in poorest physical condition.[32] The housing allowance may therefore hasten the removal of the worst housing structures from the existing housing stock (some of which might be in the public sector).

Three other important factors should also be emphasized. First, the general animus in most European housing allowance systems has not been—as in the United States—to provide the low-income household with a means to find its own housing. Rather it has been basically defensive in character—to protect the economically weak household from having to give up its existing accommodation because of an unbearable rent burden.

Moreover, the public housing sector has avoided the ghettoization that has characterized much of United States public housing because low-income families have not, as a general rule, been evicted from public housing if their incomes rise above original entrance requirements.

Second, the private rental housing sector in most European countries has been steadily shrinking and deteriorating in quality because of rent regulation and the favoritism shown homeowners.[33] Consequently, the low-income household generally does not, even in practice, have a wide range of attractive alternative accommodations from which to choose.

Third, in many European countries the housing allowance has been provided, at least in part, in the form of a rent rebate. By definition, then, it becomes a subsidy tied to a specific publicly owned dwelling unit and does not provide the household with financial means to go in search of housing accommodations on the open market. Rent rebates fall short of being a pure form of housing allowance.

In Canada, Steele contends that the housing allowance threat to public housing is minimal because of three important attributes of public housing.[34] First, public housing has easy availability, especially to high-cost households (that is, households which involve above average costs to the landlord in terms of higher maintenance costs, higher turnover rates, etc.) such as single parent families, when housing is unavailable to them in the private market.

A second advantage is assured, continuing quality. Since project operating losses are government subsidized, high maintenance costs do not drive the owner into bankruptcy; nor is there danger of a change in ownership. By contrast, private landlords, faced with high unexpected interest or other expenses, may reduce maintenance expenditures or decide to sell to a new owner.

Third, public housing offers security of tenure. Only under unusual circumstances are public tenants evicted. In the private sector, there may be much uncertainty, particularly for the elderly in cities like Toronto where gentrification in older, inner city areas is taking place. In Toronto, in 1982, 34 percent of the elderly applicants for public housing gave security of tenure as their reason for wanting to move, compared to 11 percent who were being forced to move, and 29 percent who feared for physical and personal security. Security of tenure is especially important for households such as large families that have relatively high moving costs, both financial and real.

Canadian experience in British Columbia and Manitoba provinces suggests that housing allowance programs have had little impact on public housing programs. In Manitoba the list of families waiting for public housing has grown, and public housing vacancy rates have declined; the

same is true for British Columbia elderly housing. However, the reverse
has been the case in Manitoba elderly public housing; this latter
happening may be attributable to a general decline in the attractiveness of
public housing as elderly incomes have risen.

On the other hand, the income integration achieved by a quasi-housing
allowance—the rent supplement program—appears to have received general support in Canada. For example, the Ontario Housing Corporation
rent supplement program adopted in 1971 found widespread approval,
including that of private landlords. Under the program, landlords provide
for three to five years a number of units to families from public housing
waiting lists. Tenants pay the landlords a rent geared to their income. The
Ontario Housing Corporation then pays the difference between that
amount and a current market rent agreed with the landlord. No one but
the landlord and the tenant need know that a subsidy is involved. Landlords report that problems involved with rent supplement tenants have
been no greater than those with private tenants.[35]

Summary

The housing allowance approach has chalked up some impressive
achievements. It has contributed considerably to an improvement in physical living conditions, both in the short run and the long run. It has
demonstrated the ability to substantially reduce excessive rent burdens on
low-income households. It has been an effective tool in helping to accom-
plish other important national objectives, such as unifying the rental housing market, promoting social stability, and encouraging labor mobility.

NOTES

1. Gunter Schwerz, *Systems and Significance of Individual Subsidization of
Accommodation Costs in European Countries* (Bonn: Domus-Verlag, 1966), 2, 37,
43; Robert Frommes, *Problems Raised by the Individual Subsidization of Accommodation* (Hague: International Federation of Housing and Planning, 1970), 16-
17.

2. Ira S. Lowry, *Experimenting With Housing Allowances: Executive Summary*
(Santa Monica, CA: Rand Corporation, 1982), vi.

3. E. Jay Howenstine, "Private Rental Housing Abroad: Dwindling Supply
Stirs Concern," *Monthly Labor Review* (September 1981), 38-42.

4. Federal Republic of Germany, Bundesministerium fur Bauwesen, Raumordnung und Stadtebau, *Wohngeld und Mietenbericht, 1977* (Bonn: Bundesministerium fur Bauwesen, Raumordnung und Stadtebau, 1977), Tables E9, E10.

5. Hugo Priemus, *Housing Allowances in the Netherlands* (Delft: Delft
University Press, 1984), 107.

6. Clayton Research Associates, *The Impacts of Shelter Allowances* (Ottawa: Canada Mortgage and Housing Corporation, 1981), 4.

7. *See* Marion Steele's (University of Guelph) unpublished study of housing allowances for the Ontario Economic Council in 1982, Chap. 3 and Chap. 9, 4.

8. Marion Steele, "The Low Consumption Response of Canadian Housing Allowance Recipients" in, *And Where Do We Go From Here?*, ed., Janet McClain (Ottawa: Canadian Council on Social Development, 1983), 61.

9. Ricketts has contended that the British 1972 housing allowance plan was really a "limited price reduction" policy, amounting theoretically to around 60 percent. The actual outcome of the policy, however, depended on supply side considerations, particularly on the pricing of housing services. Martin Ricketts, "The Economics of the Rent Allowance," *Scottish Journal of Political Economy* (November 1976), 258.

10. Keijo Tanner, *The Finnish Housing Allowance System for Families and Single Persons as Applied in 1983* (Helsinki: National Housing Board, 1983), App. 5.

11. France, Ministere de l'Environment et du Cadre de Vie, *Current Trends and Policies in the Field of Housing, Building and Planning* (Paris: Ministere de l'Environment et du Cadre de Vie, 1978) 14-15.

12. Federal Republic of Germany, Ministry for Regional Planning, Housing Affairs and Municipal Planning, *Housing Allowance and Rent: 1983 Report* (Germantown, MD: HUD USER, 1983), 31.

13. British Columbia, Ministry of Municipal Affairs and Housing, *Profile of the SAFER Beneficiaries* (Vancouver: Ministry of Municipal Affairs and Housing, 1978), 2.

14. Hugo Priemus, *op. cit.*, 95.

15. South Australian Housing Trust, *The Rent Relief Scheme in South Australia: The First Twelve Months* (Adelaide: South Australian Housing Trust, 1984), 7.

16. Ira S. Lowry, *op. cit.*, vi.

17. Michael Dennis and Susan Fish, *Programs in Search of a Policy: Low Income Housing in Canada* (Toronto: Hakkert, 1972), 357. *See also* A. A. Nevitt, *Housing, Taxation and Subsidies* (London: Nelson, 1966), 154; David Donnison, *The Government of Housing* (London: Penguin, 1967), 264-65; International Federation of Housing and Planning, Committee on Rent and Family Income, *Rent and Family Income* (Hague: International Federation of Housing and Planning, 1970), 56; U. Pfeiffer and K. Stahl, *Housing Finance Policies in Germany* (Bonn: Ministry for Regional Planning, Building and Urban Development, 1975); Association of Municipalities of Ontario, *Shelter Allowances* (Ontario: Association of Municipalities of Ontario, 1980), 9.

18. Lucien Wynen, *Le Financement du Logement Social* (Brussels: International Union of Family Organizations, 1962), 3-4; Association of Municipalities of Ontario, *op. cit.*, 9.

19. Canada, Canada Mortgage and Housing Corporation, *Some Considerations for Interdepartmental Task Force on Shelter Allowances* (Ottawa: Canada Mortgage and Housing Corporation, 1979), Background Document Sec. 4, 4.3.

20. International Federation for Housing and Planning, Committee on Rent and Family Income, *op. cit.*, 56.

21. Steele, *op. cit.*, Chap. 9, 3.

22. Drawn from unpublished study of Marion Steele, *op. cit.*, Chap. 7, 28.

23. *Ibid.*

24. South Australian Housing Trust, *op. cit.,* 10-11.

25. Clayton Research Associates, *op. cit.,* 4, 7. *See also* the simulation study of Frank T. Denton, A. Leslie Robb, and Byron G. Spencer, *The Economics of Shelter Allowances* (Ottawa: Canada Mortgage and Housing Corporation, 1982).

26. C. Peter Rydell and C. Lance Barnett, "Price Effects of Housing Allowances" in *The Great Housing Experiment,* eds., Joseph Friedman and Daniel H. Weinberg (Beverly Hills, CA: Sage Publications, 1983), Urban Affairs Annual Reviews, Vol. 24, 186.

27. Raymond J. Struyk, Neil Mayer, and John A. Tuccillo, *Federal Housing Policy at President Reagan's Midterm* (Washington, D.C.: Urban Institute, 1983), 72.

28. United Nations, Economic Commission for Europe, Committee on Housing, Building and Planning, *Financing of Housing* (Geneva, 1973), 19.

29. W. Weiswel, *Housing Allowances and the Dutch Rent Subsidy Program* (Santa Monica, CA: Rand Corporation, 1979), 8.

30. South Australian Housing Trust, *op. cit.,* 6-8.

31. This view has been put forward by three Canadian housing experts—Striech, Harding, and Clarke. Cited by Marion Steele, unpublished study, *op. cit.,* Chaps. 8, 27.

32. Hugo Priemus, *op. cit.,* 107.

33. E. Jay Howenstine, "Rental Housing in Industrialized Countries: Issues and Policies," in *Rental Housing: Is There a Crisis?,* eds., John C. Weicher, Kevin E. Villani, and Elizabeth A. Roistacher (Washington, D.C.: Urban Institute, 1981), 103-107.

34. Marion Steele, unpublished study, *op. cit.,* Chap. 8.

35. Laura Golob, "Rent Supplement—Everyone Likes It—Including the Private Landlords," *Housing Ontario* (June 1975), 2-4.

10

Consumer Subsidy Approach Versus Producer Subsidy Approach

One of the foremost issues in European housing subsidy policy is: Should financial assistance to low-income families be in the form of consumer housing subsidies or producer housing subsidies, or in some synthesis of the two systems?[1]

A judicious judgment on this issue cannot be reached without weighing the two systems by certain basic measures. This chapter analyzes the relative advantages and disadvantages of the consumer and producer housing subsidy approaches in the light of the following nine criteria:

1. Improving physical living conditions;
2. reducing the rent burden;
3. minimizing housing costs;
4. ensuring equity among households;
5. promoting freedom of choice in abode;
6. promoting an efficient use of the housing stock;
7. protecting the real value of the housing subsidy;
8. administrative simplicity; and
9. political viability.

Physical Living Conditions

Broadly speaking, the *raison d'être* of housing subsidies is to improve living conditions. How do these two subsidy systems compare in their impact on physical living conditions?

Low-income households required three major types of improvements in living conditions: the supply of dwelling units had to be increased to lessen overcrowding; the quality of the housing stock had to be raised so that all households occupy a decent home; and the quality and amenities of the neighborhood needed to be improved and preserved so as to ensure a livable environment.

As regards the first requirement, the European producer subsidy systems directly addressed the problem of housing shortages. The two main forms of producer subsidy have been: capital grants; and below-market interest rates on capital invested. Such subsidies have financed housing built by national, state, and local governments; quasi-governmental organizations; nonprofit organizations; cooperatives; trade unions; and individuals. By their very nature producer housing subsidies create new housing units and rehabilitate existing units. They have produced a visible increase in the supply of minimum standard dwelling units.

The producer subsidy system is also a powerful tool for improving the living environment; frequently, if not generally, the system involves building a whole new neighborhood. If projects are well designed both from the architectural and the urban points of view, and if their tenant composition has a good social mix, then this system can have a direct, positive influence on living conditions. The system also facilitates meeting certain social objectives, such as accommodation of target need groups like the elderly, or reintroduction of family oriented housing in the inner city, as has been done with Le Broton flats in Ottawa, Canada, or the St. Lawrence Development in Toronto, Canada.[2]

On the other hand, social housing programs financed by producer subsidies have on occasion not been well designed. In the pressure to economize on scarce land, projects have sometimes involved excessive use of high-rise construction, e.g., in France, the Federal Republic of Germany, the Netherlands, Sweden, and the United Kingdom.[3] In searching for available land, projects have been forced into fringe suburban locations which often lacked services, infrastructure, and public transportation.[4] Moreover, as in the case of Canada, France, and the United Kingdom, building big projects for low-income families sometimes resulted in segregation of poor families with stigma attached to them.[5]

The effect of the consumer subsidy system on the supply of housing is much less clear. As indicated in Chapter 9, Physical Living Conditions, the impact of the housing allowance system on the quantity and quality of housing has, on the whole, been relatively passive and indirect. This is equally true of its role in improving neighborhood quality.

Summarizing, there is practically unanimous agreement among European governments that the producer housing subsidy system has much the greater impact in improving physical living conditions.

Rent Burden

Historically, the price of decent housing has been beyond the reach of workers. In modern parlance, this is the problem of affordability: good housing costs more than the low-income worker can pay. What has been the relative effectiveness of the two subsidy systems in making housing affordable?

In the early post-World War II period, European producer housing subsidy systems dealt very well with the affordability problem. Since by definition they involved a deep subsidy, they brought rents down to a reasonable level for families occupying public housing.

In the last decade, however, the practicability of the deep producer subsidy has been undermined by rapidly rising housing costs. In many countries, rents of new subsidized housing rose to levels beyond the reach of the low-income family, with the result that the housing allowance was used increasingly to help government authorities clear the market of vacant dwellings.

By contrast, one of the primary inspirations behind the housing allowance has been to bring the shelter-to-income ratio down to a reasonable level. As indicated in Chapter 9, Rent Burden, most programs have been reasonably successful in achieving this objective.

Housing Costs

In the pre-World War II era, there was comparative price stability not only in the economy at large but also in the building industry. The cost structure of the national housing stock of most Western European countries, therefore, had a certain linear character over time. After World War II, however, this tranquillity was shattered as general inflationary pressures continued to push up the consumer's price index, and as special factors, particularly the rising costs of land and capital, pushed up housing costs even more.

After two decades of escalating housing costs, from 1946 to 1966, a significant gap began to emerge between the rent levels of new housing and those of existing housing. This posed a serious dilemma for European housing subsidy policies. If the expansion rate in the social housing stock and the producer housing subsidy system were regarded as constants, then the only recourse was to increase substantially total annual housing subsidies. If, however, total annual housing subsidies and the producer housing subsidy system were constants, then the only alternative was to cut back the level of new social housing construction. But, if total annual housing subsidies and the expansion rate in the social housing stock were constants, then the form of subsidy policy had to be changed, for example, by acquisition of properties from the existing privately owned housing stock built at a much lower cost level or by a consumer housing subsidy policy.

As long as European economies enjoyed high rates of national economic growth during the 1950s, 1960s, and early 1970s, it was politically and economically possible to increase annual public investments in housing without too much difficulty. But during the late 1970s and early 1980s not only did economic growth rates decline but the cost of subsidizing new workers' housing accelerated. As financial burdens on the public treasury became increasingly onerous, new policy directions became more pressing. One of these policy options was to shift more and more to housing allowances.

The consumer housing subsidy approach possessed two significant cost advantages. In the first place, payments were, for the most part, made to families living in existing housing rather than to those moving into new housing; thus, housing allowances were geared mainly to the low cost level of the existing housing stock rather than to the high cost level of new construction (although of course the reverse of this was true in some systems, such as those of Denmark and the Netherlands). Consequently, the amount of subsidy required to bring the rent for a specific family down to an affordable level tended to be considerably less under the consumer housing subsidy approach than under the producer housing subsidy approach.

In reality, governments were utilizing a considerable portion of the existing private housing stock for social housing purposes without going through all the difficult financial and organizational problems of acquiring it for the public domain and then renting it to needy families. While attracted to the concept of public acquisition or leasing of private sector housing for social housing programs, Dennis and Fish recognized the formidable difficulties of implementation.[6]

A second cost advantage emerged from the obligatory versus the permissive character of the two systems. In the producer housing subsidy system, a deep subsidy, that is, a large amount of subsidy per family, was obligatory. No half-way subsidy would get the house built; but, once it was built, it became a fixed arrangement. In the consumer housing subsidy system, however, subsidy size and scope were permissive. The subsidy could be deep, moderate, or shallow, depending on the amount of subsidy paid per family. Having this variability, a certain total national subsidy expenditure could be divided among a large, medium, or small number of households.

The cost differentials between the producer subsidy and the consumer subsidy systems can be substantial. In the Federal Republic of Germany, for example, the annual subsidy per participating household in the new public housing construction program in 1975 was estimated to be 4.5 times as high as in the housing allowance program, which was geared to the much lower original cost levels of the existing housing stock.[7] In a comparable cost comparison of U.S. housing subsidy programs, Mayo found that from two to three times as many households could be served per dollar expenditure on housing allowances as could be served by either public housing programs or by the Section 236 producer housing subsidy program.[8]

A comparative study of the cost-effectiveness of housing allowances and producer subsidy programs in Australia showed that (without taking into account capital gains), respectively, 132 households could be assisted per A$1 million of expenditure in single dwelling units in public housing programs, 105 households in attached houses in public housing programs, 143 households in purchases of existing housing for the public housing program, and 286 households in the housing allowance program. Twice the number of households could, therefore, be assisted per A$1 million of cost by the housing allowance method than by the most efficient producer subsidy system. Even if long-term capital gains of, say, 4 percent, were factored into the costs of producer subsidy programs, housing allowances were still the least costly means of providing assistance.[9]

A Canadian Task Force on Shelter and Incomes emphasized the importance of making cost comparisons in arriving at policy decisions on producer and consumer subsidy housing programs.[10] It proposed a methodology for making these comparisons between various producer subsidy systems and a housing allowance, but only cost data on producer subsidy systems were analyzed.[11]

The cost advantages have, in turn, involved significant political advantages. The housing allowance system enabled governments to make a much more creditable showing of responsiveness to meeting national housing needs than was possible under the producer housing subsidy system. That is, governments could obtain the prestige of providing a larger number of people with financial assistance (though admittedly in smaller amounts) than was possible under the producer housing subsidy system. Moreover, being much more flexible, the housing allowance could more easily expand during fiscal surplus periods or contract during periods of fiscal deficit (although from the standpoint of a compensatory full employment policy, the flexibility should be in precisely the opposite manner).

The above use of the consumer housing subsidy policy is not without a certain kind of trickery, however. Some of the visible superiority in terms of number of people served by the subsidy system may be more apparent than real. A thin distribution of the total available subsidy expenditures may mean merely that the shelter-to-income ratio has not been sufficiently reduced really to lighten the rent burden by a significant amount. If, on the other hand, a deep subsidy were adopted so as to eliminate completely the excessive rent burden for all low-income households, it would be very expensive—prohibitively so for some governments at this stage of social development and fiscal capacity.

Schwerz suggests still another long-term cost advantage of the housing allowance system. In the future when physical housing needs have been met and the vast majority of people are living in decent housing, he maintains that governments should limit housing subsidies to individual hardship cases. In this manner, each household would be encouraged to provide for itself rather than to lean on the government, thus making outmoded the historical concept that housing was primarily to be financed and built by the state.[12]

Summarizing, European experience has shown that the per participant cost of the consumer subsidy approach is considerably less than that of the producer subsidy approach. This is one of the main factors in its favor.

Equity Among Households

Equity—that is, the treatment of all households alike—is a basic objective of all public policy. In the field of housing allowances, equity is of two kinds: horizontal and vertical. Horizontal equity involves equal treatment for all households at a given income level. Vertical equity requires relatively equal treatment among households at different income levels.

Inequitable treatment of low-income households has been one of the major objections to the producer housing subsidy system. The fact is that no national construction industry has the capacity to build overnight the amount of social housing required to meet the needs of all low-income families. As Dennis and Fish pointed out, it would have been physically impossible for the Canadian construction industry to build in one year the 2.5 million dwelling units required in 1972 for all families to have decent housing. Nor were sufficient funds available for more than a limited annual construction program. National housing policy would have done well to construct the 2.5 million houses over a period of 10 years.[13]

This reality means that, at best, during any given period of time only a small percentage of low-income families can be housed by newly constructed public housing. The situation has, in fact, been likened to a lottery.[14] Moreover, while national public housing programs may minister to the most needy families at the moment of entry, with the passage of time, the families often cease to be the neediest and frequently become a kind of "privileged sector."[15] Thus, although being bountiful to those who obtain occupancy of the social housing, the system can hardly avoid a certain built-in discriminatory treatment toward those households that are not able to share in the bounty.

Moreover, as a consequence of strong emotional attachment of the family to its home, housing in Europe has involved a greater social obligation upon the part of the government and a greater social right on the part of the family than is the case in the United States. Once occupancy of a social housing unit is assigned to a family, the family tends to remain there—even from generation to generation in some cases—unless it chooses to move. Consequently, in the course of time, there have been tendencies, first, for family income to exceed the original limits of eligibility for obtaining social housing, and, second, for communities to acquire a more balanced social mix of families than has ever been possible in public housing communities in the United States.

European housing experts have estimated that in various countries 20 to 50 percent of all social housing is occupied by families who no longer meet the income eligibility requirements which pertained at the time of their entry.[16] This means, therefore, that the rent of a large number of occupants is well below what is generally regarded as a reasonable shelter-to-income ratio, i.e., 15 to 20 percent. For example, in the Federal Republic of Germany, in 1965, 73 percent of the occupants of dwellings constructed after 1948 and financed by public authorities devoted less than 15 percent of their income to rent, and 39 percent of them less than 10 percent. The Dutch Housing Needs Survey of 1964 revealed that 25 to 30 percent of the occupants of social housing had incomes above the ceilings applicable to social insurance.[17] In the Netherlands, in 1967, 78 percent of the families in social housing devoted less than 15 percent of their income to rent, and 44 percent devoted less than 10 percent.[18] With a considerable part of the social housing stock in many countries not occupied by families in greatest need, a widespread feeling has developed that the basic objective of housing subsidies has been diluted under the producer subsidy system. In all fairness, however, it must be pointed out that the above developments are attributable more to the system of social housing administration than to the producer subsidy principle itself.

Another related deficiency is the great divergence that has developed between family size and dwelling size in social housing financed by the producer housing subsidy system. Children grow up and leave home; with a smaller household, parents no longer need large accommodations. But, instead of moving to smaller quarters and making large apartments available to young couples with children, older couples tend to retain their housing because of the low rents. Thus, tenant households tend to adjust to the level of rents rather than to the size of dwelling units, which is not an efficient use of scarce housing space.

By contrast, housing allowances are generally designed so that all families at a given income level receive approximately the same treatment. If a large amount of financial assistance is politically acceptable, then much, if not all, of the excessive rent burden may be eliminated. If only a moderate amount of tax revenue can be raised for housing subsidies, then much less of the excessive rent burden is taken off the shoulders of the low-income families. But, however much is available under the housing allowance system, it tends to be distributed on equal terms among all households in a given income bracket.

By the same token, the housing allowance system is able to maintain rough equity for all income groups during periods of financial retrenchment. If, for example, in order to cope with internal recession or international balance of payments problems a government reduces its financial subsidies, the reduction can be applied across the board so as to avoid discrimination against any group of families.

It is quite possible, too, that a government may suddenly decide to increase greatly the scale of housing subsidies, for example, when President Mitterrand increased the social housing budget by 34 percent when he came to office in France in 1981. The housing allowance has the big advantage of being able to be increased quickly in the short term, whereas the producer subsidy system requires a long lead-time to substantially increase the level of output.[19]

Vertical equity is a much more complex issue, but many, if not most, housing allowance systems incorporated the principle of progressivity into their housing allowance formulas. That is, the income devoted to rent varies directly with the level of income (see Chapter 3, Shelter-to-Income Ratio).

Clearly, consumer housing subsidy systems are much more equitable to low-income households than producer housing subsidy systems.

Freedom of Choice

Increasingly in the affluent society it is being accepted that not only does every family have a right to a decent house, it also has a right to choose its place of abode. How do the two systems compare in the latter respect?

For several decades, religious, humanitarian, and trade union groups in Western Europe attacked the philosophical and social basis of the producer housing subsidy approach. Critics maintain that the fundamental objective of housing subsidies should be to minister directly to those in greatest need. Housing assistance should subsidize not inanimate "bricks and mortar," but the families who inhabit the bricks and mortar. Instead of being fixed, general, impersonal, anonymous, and tied to the building structure, housing subsidies should be flexible, personalized, portable, and tied directly to the poor family.[20] When the amount of the subsidy is tied to the house and not to the family, this creates a strong disincentive to move as households change in composition and relative need. For example, families stay on in large, low-rent, inner-city apartments long after children have grown up and left home because they cannot carry the favorable subsidy arrangements they have enjoyed for decades to another apartment. While tenant exchange plans have been of some value in enabling families to swap dwelling units within the social housing sector without losing subsidy rights, by and large the individual household has only a choice between public housing and market housing which is beyond its means. Public housing may be inappropriately located, poorly designed, or badly managed, but a household may hesitate to move, lest it lose its favorable subsidy arrangements.

By contrast, the housing allowance system gives the household a new freedom (at least in principle) to find housing of its own choosing. Continued receipt of the housing subsidy is no longer dependent on occupying a particular subsidized dwelling unit. With financial assistance geared to its income, the household can compete for and find housing space—always, of course, within the reasonable rent levels described in Chapter 3, Rent Ceiling, and within the available supply of housing. A Canadian Task Force attached special importance to this consideration as a means of avoiding "big housing projects (which) have become ghettos of the poor."[21] The Barre Commission also concluded that "The greatest merit of assistance based on the individual case is that it married the Nation's effort towards social solidarity with a respect for the liberty of individuals."[22]

The degree to which housing allowance recipients actually used this new freedom to move to a better living environment is not altogether clear. In most systems housing allowances have been conceived primarily as a defensive, rather than an offensive, strategy. That is, they have been adopted as a shield to protect families from being forced to leave existing homes and look for cheaper accommodations because of rising rents and falling incomes rather than as a new means to go and find better housing. By reducing excessive rent burdens, housing allowances made existing accommodations affordable.

The use of new freedom is also dependent on the relative tightness of the housing market. If the vacancy rate is high, there will be a greater tendency to move to better-managed housing in a better location than if the rate is low.

Age and employment characteristics are additional factors affecting freedom and mobility. Young families looking toward better job opportunities in new growth industries and areas will find a portable housing allowance of greater assistance in finding new housing elsewhere than the requirement that they find housing financed by a producer housing subsidy. On the other hand, senior citizens and ethnic groups may be more interested in remaining in familiar surroundings, close to their network of friends, than in searching for a new environment that may be superior in other respects. For the latter groups of people, the housing allowance has the advantage of being "nondisruptive."[23]

In the United States, as regards racial segregation, there have been both hopes and fears that neighborhoods' economic and social composition would be changed if EHAP removed barriers to economic and racial segregation. Although minority neighborhoods were marginally net exporters to integrated neighborhoods, relatively little change took place. Why? William Hamilton points out that many people did not want to participate in the program; that many who did participate stayed in dwellings they occupied; and that EHAP recipients who did move chose locations that were largely indistinguishable from what they would have chosen without the subsidy.[24]

As income levels rise as a result of national economic growth, and as housing markets generally become more efficient in meeting consumer needs, the likelihood is that the housing allowance will become less defensive in nature and more offensive as a tool for helping low-income households to improve their housing position.

In short, as regards promoting freedom of choice, the housing allowance has not only a clear ideological superiority over the producer housing subsidy approach, but in the course of time it will undoubtedly have greater practical advantages.

Use of Housing Stock

It is of prime importance to eliminate wasteful underutilization of the existing housing stock. First, such action helps to minimize the social deprivation suffered by low-income households continually confronted with shortages of decent housing. Second, it helps to lighten the increasingly heavy housing subsidy demands on the public treasury.

Within the framework of European housing policies, it is generally agreed that an efficient allocation of housing resources can only be achieved if rents are set at levels that cover all costs. How do the two subsidy systems measure up in this regard?

Historically, the objective of the producer subsidy approach has been to bring rents down to the capacity of low-income families to pay. This is not an "economic rent," its critics contend, but an "artificially reduced rent."[25] The dangers of pricing housing space below its real cost are twofold. First, a household has an incentive to hang on to that dwelling unit even though its housing needs may have diminished, e.g., as a result of children growing up and leaving home. This pricing principle has in fact been one of the major contributors to a distortion of postwar rental markets between the "haves" (that is, the long-standing occupants) and the "have-nots" (the recent tenants).

Second, it pressures the legislative body to appropriate more funds for the housing sector than may really be warranted if proper account is taken of other competing high priority needs of the society. Accordingly, it is contended (in a somewhat exaggerated manner) that "in the final analysis, such a policy will only end in paralyzing the private rental housing market, in sterilizing the initiative of private capital, in intensifying the housing shortage and in bankrupting the Government."[26]

By comparison, the housing allowance approach works the other way around. It accepts the costs and the market rents of housing as constants and brings otherwise unaffordable housing within the reach of low-income households by supplementing their incomes. "Economic rents" are charged, and housing space is allocated efficiently in terms of consumer needs.

As a matter of fact, as indicated in Chapter 2, several governments, notably Denmark, Ireland, the Netherlands, Norway, and the United Kingdom, employed the housing allowance as a tool to achieve more efficient use of housing space by helping to harmonize rent levels following the relaxation of rent controls in the 1960s.

In 1967 Denmark embarked on a policy of, on the one hand, raising rents by one-eighth a year, and, on the other hand, introducing a housing allowance for low-income families to keep the shelter-to-income ratio within the 20 percent range—particularly for persons who had no alternative to moving into new housing built at high-cost levels. The Netherlands adopted a similar policy in 1970 of raising rents at the annual rate of 4 percent (later increased to 6 percent) while reducing annual interest subsidies by an equivalent amount. To relieve hardships on individuals whose incomes were not rising commensurately, the Dutch government adopted a housing allowance. In 1972 the United Kingdom adopted a policy of introducing a "fair rent" for all public and private rental housing. The resulting higher rents were met partly by substituting a housing allowance system based on individual family need for the traditional producer subsidy system based on below-market interest rates. In 1973 the Norwegian government increased its housing allowance substantially to overcome individual hardships, particularly for the elderly, resulting from the raising of rents following relaxation of rent controls and the raising of mortgage interest rates on older housing.

The consensus of European opinion seems to be that the consumer housing subsidy system leads to much more effective use of the existing housing stock.

Real Value of the Housing Subsidy

An important factor to weigh in comparing the two subsidy systems is their relative ability to resist erosion in the real value of the housing subsidy. For example, if financial assistance to low-income families is absorbed in whole or in part by rent increases, the household may be little, if any, better off than before.

The producer subsidy system has high resistance to erosion in both the short and long term. The assistance—being the lever by which the dwelling comes into existence—becomes an integral part of the original financial structure and is thereby translated into the rent schedule. Save in exceptional circumstances, the occupant enjoys the subsidized rent indefinitely.

The housing allowance recipient is not so well protected. As discussed in Chapter 9, Housing Allowance Strategies, in a private rental housing market free of rent regulations, there is the risk that the landlord may capture all or a part of the allowance in the form of rent increases, depending on such factors as the vacancy rate, the size of the allowance, and the number of participants in any local housing market. In the public rental market, there is no such risk.

In practice, there appears to have been comparatively little inflation of rents by European landlords as housing allowances were introduced, because of, first, the existence of some sort of rent regulation in most urban centers, and, second, the large size of the public housing sector. This may not have been equally true of Canada, and perhaps Australia, where mainly uncontrolled housing markets exist.

Summarizing, the producer housing subsidy system offers more assurance than the consumer housing subsidy system that the financial assistance will be protected against rent inflation.

Administrative Simplicity

To ensure that financial assistance goes to the most needy in both producer and consumer housing subsidy systems, most governments require that applicants pass means tests. Means tests are, however, notorious. They invade family privacy, they create tensions within multiadult households, they have serious disincentive effects, and they are difficult to administer fairly. But if there are no means tests, how is it possible to achieve equity among households with differing numbers of wage earners, different numbers of children, and different incomes?[27]

Administratively, the major differences between the two subsidy systems come after the initial application of the means test. In the case of producer housing subsidy systems, the European practice generally has been that the family remains in the dwelling unit until it wants to move. Eviction is seldom required if household income rises and exceeds minimum eligibility entrance requirements; hence there is little need to monitor changes in household income. Nor is there need for inspection of premises to enforce minimum housing standards; these standards are assured under the public ownership system. The subsidy arrangements are regularized by the central government from the beginning and normally remain unchanged.

In the housing allowance, on the other hand, the approach is quite different. The shelter-to-income ratio is the core concept. If both rent and income—and, in addition, family size—are independent variables, then the subsidy is inherently unstable. If the shelter-to-income ratio is declining (that is, if the rent burden falls), then the housing allowance is reduced. If the ratio increases (that is, if the situation worsens), the housing allowance is increased. This seems simple and all very well. But administratively it is immensely complicated. It requires continuous surveillance of changes in the income, rent, and persons of each household.[28]

Administratively, most housing allowance systems are more complicated than the producer subsidy system. On-site inspection is required if one condition is that the participant live in a minimum standard dwelling. Moreover, many systems prohibit the renting of an excessive amount of space; this also requires administrative follow-up. The reality is that the greater the sophistication in establishing an equitable housing allowance system, the more difficult and expensive the system is to administer. Yet without the sophistication, programs tend to be inadequate and inequitable.[29]

The housing allowance system admits to two types of administrative simplification. First, Sweden and Austria adopted a highly simplified administrative setup using the income tax system. In Sweden each household that qualifies on the basis of the information in its tax return automatically receives an application for a housing allowance along with instructions on how to fill out the form. This procedure ensures an effective preliminary screening of households from the standpoint of potential need. Nevertheless, the 20-month time lag between receipt of taxable income data and of current income data does create minor equity problems. In order to keep administrative costs low, the housing allowance is not subject to upward or downward adjustment until the change exceeds 25 percent.[30] Consequently, since most household incomes tend to rise, the time lag results in small overpayments by government and small underpayments for some households. Sweden and Austria have kept their administrative costs to between 3 and 5 percent.

A second type of simplification has been proposed by Dennis and Fish. The idea is to pay all eligible households an amount equal to the difference between one-fifth of average annual income for households within that income group and the rental cost of an average adequate unit for a household of that size. Payment would be made in advance on receipt of proof of income by way of tax receipt. Such a system would have administrative simplicity, low administrative cost, lack of controls, and universal participation. It would have the advantage, too, of easy conversion into a guaranteed annual income program, if that were the ultimate national objective.[31]

Such a proposal has significant drawbacks, however. It loses the direct connection between the housing allowance and housing improvement. It deals in averages and treats low-income tenants the same as low-income owners. It ignores differences in living costs arising from size and location of cities and towns, and from different cost structures in urban centers of the same size. The administrative neatness, therefore, comes only with the sacrifice of equity.

Taking all factors into consideration, it is generally agreed that the producer housing subsidy system is the easier of the two systems to administer.

Political Viability

One final criterion to be considered is political viability: Other things being equal, which subsidy approach will rally the greatest amount of popular support in the long run?

By actually building new housing and community facilities, the producer subsidy system has the advantage of yielding visible evidence of good results. Moreover, the industries and occupations which are involved in new construction, such as the building industry, the building materials and equipment industries, real estate developers, building trades unions, architects, and engineers, all are, of course, strong supporters of the producer subsidy systems.

However, as observed above, new construction does not always end with a felicitous conclusion. Public housing has sometimes resulted in segregation and ghettos of the poor, which in turn have alienated the citizenry against public housing programs.

Housing allowances, on the other hand, have a measurable effect in lowering the rent burden of the low-income households but contribute little direct stimulus to the building of new housing. Moreover, while most housing allowance recipients in European programs have continued to live in existing abodes, the financial assistance is commonly portable and thus facilitates the dispersion of low-income families throughout the existing housing stock. This minimizes segregation.

At the same time, however, the housing allowance is generally used not to increase the quality of housing but to reduce the rent burden. Consequently, some of the citizenry, seeing the effects of the reduced rent burden taking the form of increased consumer expenditure, for example, purchasing better quality food for the family, have taken a narrow-minded view that the purpose of the housing allowance is being subverted and that, therefore, the subsidy should be withdrawn.

One of the special advantages of the housing allowance is that it has a built-in mechanism for automatic phasing out. As family income rises, the amount of the allowance decreases until the income ceiling is reached, and the allowance is terminated. Presumably rising family income means declining family need, but this may not at all be the case. If the rise in income is real, that is, if it is associated with occupational advancement and rising productivity, then the need for subsidy steadily diminishes. But the rise may be in money terms, not in real terms, and because of inflation the family may be no better off than before. To deal with this problem, governments need to raise income eligibility ceilings in accordance with the rate of inflation.

By contrast, there is no automatic phasing out of the producer housing subsidy. At the time of construction, the government normally takes on a fixed subsidy commitment for the reasonable life of the dwelling unit (that is, for the duration of the subsidized loan).

The flexibility of the housing allowance finance mechanism may, on the other hand, leave recipients highly vulnerable; in times of fiscal distress housing allowance programs are easy to turn off just as in times of financial abundance they can be easily expanded. By comparison, while current producer housing subsidy programs financing new building projects can be turned off in a similar way, those which are financing existing housing cannot be turned off because they involve long-term government debt obligations.[32]

Summarizing, all things considered, there seems to be little preference between the two systems in regard to political viability.

Striking the Balance

Tallying up the contest between the two subsidy systems, the consumer subsidy approach wins in regard to five criteria: reducing the excessive rent burden; minimizing housing costs; ensuring equity; promoting freedom of choice of abode; and promoting efficient use of the existing housing stock. The producer subsidy approach has the advantage in regard to three criteria: improving housing conditions; protecting the value of the housing subsidy; and administrative simplicity. And as regards the ninth criterion—political viability—the result is more or less a draw.

The above results might seem to suggest that the consumer housing subsidy is the superior approach. Such a conclusion would, however, seem overly simplistic and misleading.

A fair assessment of the two approaches can only be made with relation to conditions in the current housing market. The crucial question is: How adequate is the existing quantity and quality of housing? If there is a serious housing shortage in the country as a whole, in a particular locality or region, or in a particular segment of the housing market, European experience indicates that the producer housing subsidy system is the most effective tool for dealing with the shortage. Even such a vigorous consumer subsidy proponent as Lucien Wynen concedes that producer subsidies are required, first, when there is a critical housing shortage, and, second, when a slum clearance effort is called for.[33]

But if there is no severe housing supply problem, and if the major problem is the excessive rent burden on low-income families, then there may be a firm basis for placing the major thrust of national policy on the consumer housing subsidy approach. The facts are, however, that all foreign governments, regardless of their policy declarations, have found a continuing need for both types of subsidies; futhermore, most have devoted more financial resources to producer types of subsidy than to housing allowances (see Chapter 8, Table 11).

Several European governments have made major policy changes that are instructive on this issue. In 1968 the Swedish government switched from producer housing subsidies to consumer housing subsidies on the belief that the national backlog of housing need had been basically overcome. This did not mean, however, that the government intended to rely solely on housing allowances to stimulate new housing production. Rather, it simultaneously introduced a nonsubsidy production incentive system in the form of a lenient mortgage repayment system in the early years of the mortgage. However, the latter system encountered great difficulties because of, among other things, unanticipated changes in building costs and interest rates. Over the years the fact is that emphasis has gradually shifted back to the producer subsidy approach, until in 1981 housing allowances at $1.2 billion (SK6 billion) were the smallest of the subsidy programs—compared to $1.4 billion (SK7.2 billion) for interest subsidies, and $2.3 billion (SK11.5 billion) for tax subsidies to owner-occupiers (Table 11).

An eminent national commission, under Raymond Barre, was appointed in France in 1975 to examine the housing subsidy system. The commission concluded that the existing producer subsidy system was wasteful, inflexible, costly, and inequitable; and, it proposed that eventually the producer subsidy system should be largely replaced by the consumer housing subsidy system.[34] Following the commission's recommendations, in 1977 a major reform in the housing allowance system (l'aide personnalisee au logement) was put into operation on an experimental basis with the declared objective that over the next 10-year period consumer housing subsidies would rise from one-third to two-thirds of the total national housing subsidy expenditures.[35] Construction subsidies were simultaneously reduced through changes in the loan system. Nevertheless, over the years producer-type subsidies have continued to play the dominant role in national housing policy. In 1984 housing allowances were approximately $1.5 billion (FF12.4 billion), constituting only one-fifth of total housing subsidies, with direct producer subsidies amounting to $2.5 billion (FF19.7 billion) and tax concessions (in 1982—later figures not available) amounting to $3 billion (FF24.5 billion; Table 11).

The Dutch government likewise adopted a long-term policy giving great prominence to the consumer housing subsidy approach. In 1974 the Housing Advisory Committee issued an authoritative report recommending major changes on a number of points. The scope of the housing allowance should be extended to all rented dwellings, doubling the persons covered to around 300,000. The shelter-to-income ratios should be progressive, ranging (in 1975) from 10 percent for persons (e.g., pensioners and families on welfare) below the minimum wage of $5,535 (FL14,000) to 18.8 percent for persons with taxable incomes of $9,885 (FL25,000). Young persons living alone should be covered. Housing allowances should be integrated with a rent regulation system covering practically the whole rental sector. The housing allowance should be based solely on incomes and rents; dwelling size, household size, dwelling quality, etc., should no longer be considered. Producer subsidies should be designed to bring the rents of new housing down to a reasonable level. The recommendations were generally accepted by the government and became the basis of a thorough overhaul of the housing allowance system. The new regulations introduced on July 1, 1975, envisaged a steady increase in both housing allowance recipients and expenditures under a system of mixed producer and consumer subsidies.[36] In 1984 the government announced a long-term policy for the rental housing sector that would, by 1987, provide for higher expenditures on housing allowances (i.e., FL3.1 million) than on producer subsidies (FL2.9 million).[37]

In a 1977 Green Paper, the United Kingdom Department of the Environment (DOE) presented the concept of a "universal housing allowance" as a possible replacement for the current program of general and income-related housing financial assistance. This would take the form of a regular, flat-rate payment to all beneficiaries and would be large enough to enable the most hard-pressed families to afford housing of a reasonable, basic standard. But it would be subject to income tax—so that a portion could be "clawed back" from the better-off households through the workings of the tax system.

The Green Paper noted that such a system raised four practical problems:

- "It would be difficult to define eligibility in numerous border-line cases—for example, would any single adult who wishes to live independently qualify, and would those who owned their homes outright and no longer needed assistance qualify too?

- Would recipients of the allowance be free to spend it on goods other than housing, accepting a lower standard of accommodation if they preferred to do so?

- The payment of a universal allowance, with income tax clawback, would involve a very large increase in the gross flow of payments in both directions, and a clawback through the tax system would not secure full repayments from those who did not need assistance; and

- A fixed sum providing adequate help to households with heavy housing costs would be more than adequate for others with lower costs; but if set at a lower level it would be insufficient for the many households with higher than average costs."[38]

The DOE suggested that the first two objections might be overcome, although only by complex administrative mechanisms. But the last two were more difficult, especially the variation in the level of housing payments. The Green Paper concluded that because of the wide variation in housing costs and householders' payments under existing arrangements, the introduction of a consistent basis of pricing in all housing sectors—based on current market values—should be regarded as a necessary prior step to the introduction of such a universal housing allowance. No action was ever taken on this proposal.

A less favorable view toward consumer housing subsidies has been expressed in other countries. In Canada there has been a wide-ranging debate for more than 15 years concerning the desirability of adopting a comprehensive, nationwide housing allowance system. In fact, various types of "shelter allowances" have been operating for more than 10 years: at the national level as a rent supplement under the National Housing Act and as a shelter component of welfare assistance; at the provincial and municipal levels as a shelter component of welfare assistance; and as five separate provincial housing allowance systems for the elderly. The Canadian Council on Social Development convened a conference of the nation's housing organizations in November, 1978, to discuss the question: Are housing allowances the answer? The consensus was that "housing allowances are at best stop-gap measures. They solve housing affordability problems in the interim, but will never replace more comprehensive income support and publicly assisted housing programs."[39] A report of the Association of Municipalities of Ontario reached a similar view in 1980 as follows:

"A shelter allowance program can be a useful mechanism to reduce affordability problems for some people who are adequately housed or have access to adequate and appropriate housing, but it can only be one part of a package of assistance measures because of its limited scope, allowance inadequacy and lack of market sensitivity."[40]

A major international Seminar on Housing convened by the United Nations Economic Commission for Europe in 1973 arrived at similar reservations with regard to housing allowances:

"[The housing allowance approach] does not provide a means of ensuring that enough homes will be built, or of promoting improvements in the existing housing stock, or of exerting pressure on prices, or of encouraging productivity and innovation. Hence personal assistance cannot replace building assistance completely so long as shortages and inelasticities—even if only sectoral—persist."[41]

A distinct shift in favor of producer housing subsidies is to be noted among some European housing economists. The Dutch economist de Haan has maintained that the housing allowance cannot deal with factors which restrict housing supply, such as the provision of finance, and that producer subsidies are needed to stimulate new housing construction.[42] The Danish economist Sondergaard, believing that too much emphasis has been put on housing allowances, has argued for a reallocation of financial assistance from consumer to producer housing subsidies.[43] The German economist Pfeiffer has contended that producer housing subsidies, rather than housing allowances, are required to tackle the main German housing problem involving poor accommodations for low-income minorities living in central cities.[44]

In practice, it is not clear that either subsidy approach uniformly dominates national policy. Rather, the two subsidy systems appear to be regarded as basically complementary, with each approach having a special role to play.

In conclusion, it is worth noting an interesting way of integrating the two systems. That is, build the type of new housing wanted in the desired location by the producer subsidy system; then, after completion, replace producer subsidies with consumer subsidies.

Following the British 1972 Housing Finance Act pattern, it is comparatively simple to convert the financial accounting which governs existing public housing from a producer subsidy system to a consumer subsidy system. Instead of paying or extending interest subsidies to local housing authorities or nonprofit organizations to enable them to amortize their capital costs while charging low rents to tenants, the national government can gradually raise rents to the market level and supplement the income of tenants so that they can pay the increased rents. Such an arrangement enables local housing authorities and nonprofit organizations to obtain sufficient income to amortize capital costs without interest or operating subsidies.

This particular form of consumer housing subsidy is not, it should be observed, a full-bodied housing allowance; rather it is, more properly speaking, a rent rebate. It does not give the recipient portable financial assistance which can be used to go into the open housing market—public anc private—to obtain accommodation of one's choice. Moreover, it is by definition tied to the cost level of the dwelling unit at the time of construction. With current housing construction costs often running two to three times the cost levels of two or three decades earlier, such an application of the consumer housing subsidy principle immediately foregoes the cost advantages that can be obtained from a freestanding housing allowance that entitles the recipient to find suitable existing housing in the open market.

On the other hand, such a combination of the two systems retains certain advantages of the consumer subsidy system. It is geared to the concept of market rents at economic cost levels; this makes for a better long-term allocation of resources and helps preserve a more competitive relationship with the private rental housing sector. It also facilitates an automatic phasing out of the consumer housing subsidy as need diminishes, that is, as workers' real incomes gradually increase as a result of rising national productivity and personal advancement.

The 1977 French housing allowance program, l'Aide Personnalisee au Logement (APL), set out to develop a synthesis somewhat along the above lines. The government is using the housing allowance as an integral part of a broad program for not only achieving affordable rents, but also for improving the quality and increasing the quantity of the existing housing stock. Contracts are drawn up with private companies and quasi-public organizations under which credits are extended for the rehabilitation of existing housing and the construction of new housing, on the condition that dwelling units are made available for low-income families at reasonable rents. The renter pays a reasonable percent of household income as rent, and the government supplements this by paying a housing allowance directly to the public or private landlord. By June, 1981, 78,000 renters and 255,000 homeowners had enrolled in the APL; at that time program participation was expanding at a rate of 15 percent every three months, with the expectation that eventually 3 million households would be included.[45]

NOTES

1. For useful discussions of the pros and cons of the two subsidy systems *see:* United Nations Economic Commission for Europe, Committee on Housing, Building and Planning, *Financing of Housing* (Geneva: United Nations Economic Commission for Europe, 1973), 18-20; Michael Dennis and Susan Fish, *Programs in Search of a Policy: Low Income Housing in Canada* (Toronto: Hakkert, 1972), 351-60; Raymond Barre (Chairman), *Report of a Commission to Study a Reform of the Financing of Housing* (Germantown, MD: HUD USER, 1976), Chap. II; Association of Municipalities of Ontario, *Shelter Allowances* (Toronto: Association of Municipalities of Ontario, 1980), 7-8; Stephen K. Mayo and Jorn Barnbrock, *Rental Housing Subsidy Programs in Germany and the U.S.: A Comparative Program Evaluation* (Bonn: Bundesministerium fur Bauwesen, Raumordnung und Stadtebau, 1980), 7-10; Michael John Oxley, "Housing Policy in Western Europe: An Economic Analysis of the Aims and Instruments of Housing Policy in the United Kingdom, West Germany, France, the Netherlands, Denmark and Ireland" (Ph.D. diss., Leicester University, 1983), 276-79; Hugo Priemus, *Housing Allowances in the Netherlands* (Delft: Delft University Press, 1984), 111-13.
2. Association of Municipalities of Ontario, *op. cit.,* 10.
3. United Kingdom, Department of the Environment, *Housing Policy: Technical Volume* (London: HMSO, 1977), Pt. III, 186.
4. Michael Dennis and Susan Fish, *op. cit.,* 353.
5. Association of Municipalities of Ontario, *op. cit.,* 1.
6. Dennis and Fish, *op. cit.,* 353.
7. Stephen K. Mayo and Jorn Barnbrock, *op. cit.,* 37-38.
8. Stephen K. Mayo, S. Mansfield, W. D. Warner, and R. Zwetchkenbaum, *Housing Allowances and Other Rental Assistance Programs—A Comparison Based on the Housing Allowance Demand Experiment, Part 2—Costs and Efficiency* (Cambridge, MA: Abt Associates, 1980), 103.
9. Pugh and Catt, *A Cost-Benefit and Financial Analysis of Australian Public Housing Programs,* S.A.I.T., Forum Series No. 3 (1983); quoted in South Australian

Housing Trust, *The Rent Relief Scheme in South Australia: The First Twelve Months* (n.p., 1984), 8-10.

10.   Canada, Task Force on Shelter and Incomes, *Report 1* (Ottawa: Central Mortgage and Housing Corporation, 1976), 35-58.

11.   I. Lithwick, "Derivation of Costs to Government for Providing Low-Income Housing Under Alternative Programs and Assumptions" in Task Force on Shelter and Incomes, *Appendices to Report 1* (Ottawa: Central Mortgage and Housing Corporation, 1976), App. H., 55-73. For another Canadian view, *see* James A. MacMillian and Edith Nickel, "An Economic Appraisal of Urban Housing Assistance: Rental Supplements Versus Public Housing," *Canadian Public Administration*, Vol. 17 (Fall 1974), 443-60. For an Australian viewpoint, *see* S. N. Tucker, "An Analysis of Housing Subsidy Schemes in Australia," *Urban Studies*, Vol. 20 (November 1983), 439-53. For a Swedish viewpoint, *see* Lennart J. Lundquist, *Housing Tenures in Sweden* (Stockholm: National Swedish Institute for Building Research, 1981), 15 ff.

12.   Gunter Schwerz, *Systems and Significance of Individual Subsidization of Accommodation Costs in European Countries* (Bonn: Domus-Verlag, 1966), 64.

13.   Dennis and Fish, *op. cit.*, 351.

14.   Clayton Research Associates, *The Impacts of Shelter Allowances* (Ottawa: Canada Mortgage and Housing Corporation, 1981), 9.

15.   International Union of Family Organisations, *Cout du Logement et Integration du Loyer dans le Budget Familial* (Brussels: International Union of Family Organisations, 1962), 1-2.

16.   Robert Frommes, *Problems Raised by the Individual Subsidization of Accommodation* (Hague: International Federation of Housing and Planning, 1970), 6.

17.   Hugo Priemus, "Housing Costs and Ability-to-Pay: A Perspective for the Eighties," in *Who Will Pay the Housing Bill in the Eighties?*, ed., Hugo Priemus (Delft: Delft University Press, 1983), 78.

18.   International Federation of Housing and Planning, Committee on Rent and Family Income, *Rent and Family Income* (Hague: International Federation of Housing and Planning, 1970), 47.

19.   Association of Municipalities of Ontario, *op. cit.*, 7-8.

20.   International Union of Family Organisations, *Compte-Rendu, Commission du Logement* (Brussels: International Union of Family Organisations, 1962), 11-13; Frommes, *op. cit.*, 1-3; Raymond Barre (Chairman), *op. cit.*, Chap. III.

21.   Canada, Federal Task Force on Housing and Urban Development, *Report* (Ottawa: Queen's Printer, 1969), 54.

22.   Raymond Barre (Chairman), *op. cit.*, 56.

23.   Association of Municipalities of Ontario, *op. cit.*, 7.

24.   William L. Hamilton, "Economic and Racial/Ethnic Concentration," in *The Great Housing Experiment*, eds., Joseph Friedman and Daniel H. Weinberg (Beverly Hills: Sage Publications, 1983), 218.

25.   Remarks of Francois Bruntz in International Union of Family Organisations, *Compte-Rendu, op. cit.*, 11.

26.   Lucien Wynen, *Le Financement du Logement Social* (Brussels: International Union of Family Organisations, 1962), 4.

27.   J. B. Cullingworth, *Housing Allowances: The British Experience* (Toronto: Centre for Urban and Community Studies, University of Toronto, 1977), 23.

28.   United Nations Economic Commission for Europe, Committee on Housing, Building and Planning, *Financing of Housing, op. cit.*, 20.

29. Association of Municipalities of Ontario, *op. cit.*, 10.

30. K. F. Watson, F. Ermuth, and W. Hamilton, *A Comparative Analysis of Housing Allowance Programs* (Ottawa: Central Mortgage and Housing Corporation, 1978), F-23.

31. Dennis and Fish, *op. cit.*, 355.

32. *See* Judy Forrest, Policy Development Officer, City of Ottawa Non-Profit Housing Corporation, in *And Where Do We Go From Here?*, ed., Janet McClain (Ottawa: Canadian Council on Social Development, 1983), 71.

33. International Union of Family Organisations, *Compte-Rendu, Commission du Logement*, 2.

34. Raymond Barre, *op. cit.*, Chap. III.

35. France, Ministere de l'Equipement, *La Reforme du Logement* (n.p., 1977), 8.

36. Hugo Priemus, *op. cit.*, 15-20.

37. *Ibid.*, 45.

38. United Kingdom, Department of the Environment, *Housing Policy: A Consultative Document* (London: Her Majesty's Stationary Office, 1977), Cmnd. 6851, 33-34. In the United States, Edgar Olsen has argued that (1) low-income people would be better served if existing producer subsidy programs were terminated and the money used for cash transfers, and (2) if, as a national policy, poor families should be housed in better accommodations than they would be able to occupy on their own, then existing producer subsidy programs should be replaced with a universal housing allowance program. Edgar O. Olsen, "Implications for Housing Policy" in *The Great Housing Experiment, op cit.*, 273.

39. Janet McClain, ed., *Are Housing Allowances the Answer?* (Ottawa: Canadian Council on Social Development, 1979), 5.

40. Association of Municipalities of Ontario, *op. cit.*, 11.

41. United Nations Economic Commission for Europe, Committee on Housing, Building and Planning, *Financing of Housing, op. cit.*, 19.

42. R. M. de Haan, quoted in H. Priemus, *Individuele Huursubsisdie Evaluatie van een Instrument von Volkshuisvestings Beleid* (1977), British Library translation, cited in Michael John Oxley, *op. cit.*, 302.

43. J. Sondergaard, *Direct og indirect tilsud til boligsforbruget* (1978), British Library translation, "Direct and Indirect Housing Subsidies," cited in Michael John Oxley, *op. cit.*, 302.

44. U. Pfeiffer, *Housing Policy in the Affluent Society* (Bonn, 1976), cited in Michael John Oxley, *op. cit.*, 302.

45. Information provided by D. Loudenot, Director, Office of Financial and Fiscal Studies, Ministry of Urban Planning and Housing, Paris, October 20, 1981.

11

Housing Allowance Versus
General Income Maintenance Policy

Problem

One of the long-standing problems in dealing with socially deprived people in an industrial society is the extensive overlap between housing subsidies and income security systems. Income security includes the welfare system and the social insurance system for the unemployed, sick, retired, and the single parent caring for children. Welfare systems—both public and private—are designed mainly for the dependent, nonworking poor. Since all households have rent to pay, either welfare payments contain a component more or less designed to cover shelter costs, or it is assumed that welfare payments are somehow generally large enough to cover the cost of housing. Similarly, in various types of insurance such as old-age pensions, it is assumed that beneficiary payments will be generally adequate to cover costs of living, including housing costs.

The fact is, however, that income security systems often do not provide a level of income that enables poor families to obtain decent housing without incurring excessive rent burdens. To deal with this problem, housing subsidies have been developed not only to provide decent housing at affordable rents for households living in substandard accommodations, but also to eliminate the excessive rent burdens for families that are already living in decent housing. As a consequence, there is in many countries a big overlap between housing subsidies and income security systems among families living in social housing but who are also recipients of income security payments.

This overlap has led to another problem that in the United Kingdom has been referred to as the "poverty trap." Considerable work disincentives may be created if the cumulative benefits received under various income transfer programs, including housing allowances, are greater than what the recipient can earn in paid employment.

Inequities are striking. For example, in Toronto, Canada, in 1973, 70 percent of the welfare recipients living in private housing spent more for shelter than they received in shelter allowance assistance. The average shelter-to-income ratio was 41 percent, and about 40 percent lived in unsound, unsafe, and very poor housing.[1] Housing allowances can also be highly variable among different provinces within a country. For example, in the western Canadian provinces, depending on which side of the border a couple resides, they may receive in their welfare payments a shelter allowance of $40 in Saskatchewan or $165 in Alberta.[2]

A somewhat similar overlap has developed in the United Kingdom, where low-income tenants have been financially assisted with four major systems: rent rebates for public housing occupants; rent allowances for private rental housing tenants; local property tax rebates for owner-occupants and tenants; and housing payments under the social security system (called supplementary benefit system) paid out by the national Department of Health and Social Security. The disadvantages are many. Many people qualify for benefits in more than one system. But since each system has complicated methods of calculating benefits, many claimants have difficulties in choosing the "best buy." As a result, claimants are frequently changing from one system to another, involving endless administrative maneuvering and considerable dissatisfaction. There are also important inequities between the dependent poor and the working poor. Supplementary benefit payments to the dependent poor may cover all rent and property taxes, whereas housing allowances are less generous to working households living on similar incomes.[3] Approximately 3 million households—one-tenth of the population—receive housing payments as a part of supplementary benefits.

In 1980-81, investigations of supplementary benefit participants resulted in the transfer of 90,000 households from the national social security system to the housing allowance system administered by local governments. But the Advisory Committee on Rent Rebates and Rent Allowances believed there were another 270,000 people drawing housing allowances who would have been better off with social insurance benefits. In another study, it was estimated that about 400,000 people—mostly pensioners—were failing to get the housing allowance to which they were entitled.[4] The recurrent political controversy in the United Kingdom resulting from the overlap between consumer housing subsidy systems and income security systems and from the differential treatment between the working poor and the nonworking poor has led to widespread reexamination of the roles of these two approaches in national policy.

The remainder of this chapter will examine, first, the rationale of the general income support approach; second, the defense of the housing allowance approach; and finally, attempts to develop a rapprochement between the two concepts.

General Income Supports

There are several important elements in the rationale arguing for a general income maintenance plan to replace all types of transfer payments, and in particular the housing allowance.[5]

The first proposition is that in the highly industrialized European countries there is no longer a housing problem *per se*. It is conceded that, historically, the housing crisis had been a supply problem; neither the quantity nor the quality of the housing stock could ensure that a decent house was available to all families. Workers and their families had little choice but to find a niche as best they could in crowded industrial slums. In these conditions it was essential to have a vigorous housing subsidy policy to stimulate the construction of new housing and the rehabilitation and modernization of the old.

By the 1970s, however, there were no longer significant slum areas in the highly industrialized countries that needed rebuilding; nor was there an acute shortage of housing. Any remaining peripheral supply problems, it was maintained, could be handled adequately through the regular operation of market forces without a specific housing subsidy system, provided all households had enough income.

The second proposition is that the remaining major housing subsidy issue—whether the worker can afford to pay for the costs of decent housing, assuming it is available—is fundamentally an income, not a housing, problem. For example, if a worker is earning only a poverty level income or below, the person can certainly not afford as good housing as would be possible if his annual income were, say, 50 percent or 100 percent higher. Moreover, if it is deemed reasonable that a worker should pay no more than, say 10 to 15 percent of income for shelter, the person cannot afford as good housing as would be possible if the reasonable shelter-to-income ratio were set at 25 to 30 percent. In both cases it is contended that the solution is basically an income problem, that is, a shortage of income, and not a shortage of housing space. This reasoning led some experts to maintain that the affordability issue is best dealt with as a general income problem through such means as a guaranteed annual income or a negative income tax, rather than as a housing problem through some form of housing allowance.[6]

In the case of families whose incomes are totally inadequate to meet shelter and other basic cost-of-living expenditures, the housing allowance by itself will not be able to provide adequate assistance. Such families, it is maintained, have "a greater problem than housing affordability, and more broadly based income support assistance must be delivered."[7]

A Canada Mortgage and Housing Corporation study of American housing allowance experience has shown that participants tended to view housing allowances as if they were straight income transfers. Where direct comparisons were possible between income transfer experiments which were not tied to minimum housing standards and housing allowance experiments that were tied, the housing consumption effects were very similar. The elasticities of housing demand were essentially the same, ranging between .2 and .4.[8]

There has been a great amount of discussion, particularly among bodies dealing with social security problems, such as the International Social Security Association,[9] concerning the place of housing allowances in the social security system, especially in that part concerned with family benefits. In France, for example, the initial housing allowance system was regarded more as a social security benefit than a housing subsidy and was financed directly from the Family Allowance Fund rather than from a National Housing Fund. Similarly, in the British Columbia (Canada) SAFER program, the housing allowance tends to be regarded as a welfare payment to the elderly—an income support measure—as much as a housing subsidy, and it is administered by the provincial Ministry on Human Services, not by the Housing Ministry.

There has also been considerable discussion of the policy of merging the housing allowance into a more generalized system of income support of all low-income households. For example, a Commission on Social Policy in the Federal Republic of Germany concluded that tax concessions or a negative income tax would be a more effective tool for achieving redistribution of income than a housing allowance.[10] Similarly in Canada, a major conference on housing allowances convened by the Canadian Council on Social Development concluded that housing allowances are "at best stop-gap measures" and that while "they solve housing affordability problems in the interim . . . [they] will never replace more comprehensive income support and publicly assisted housing programs."[11]

Two Canadian economists, Fallis and Smith,[12] have proposed that the whole social housing program should be replaced by an income redistribution program, while the American Nobel Laureate economist, Milton Friedman, has proposed a 50 percent negative income tax as a substitute for current welfare and housing programs.[13]

The third proposition is that considerable savings in administrative costs can be achieved by abolishing the housing allowance administration and merging the system with other social benefit programs in one single minimum or guaranteed family income program.[14] As observed in Chapter 2, Elderly Hardship Model, historically from two-thirds to three-quarters of housing allowance recipients in France, the Federal Republic of Germany, Sweden, and the United Kingdom have been pensioners. It has been contended, therefore, that administratively it would be simple and efficient to combine the housing allowance with the pension system, and in the process also increase the level of participation of the needy elderly in housing assistance.

The fourth proposition is that merging the housing allowance system with a general income support program would give the worker complete freedom to spend income in accordance with preferences and thus to maximize consumer satisfaction. It is maintained that consumers know better than legislators or bureaucrats how to spend their income on housing services. If they choose to live in low-standard housing and spend more income on other goods and services, this should be their right.[15]

Housing Allowance

There is little disposition on the part of housing allowance proponents generally to deny either the proposition that the overall housing shortage has been largely eliminated as a result of the massive house building programs since World War II or the proposition that the principal housing problem is one of affordability, that is, a lack of income to pay the costs of decent housing. But it is argued that there are cogent reasons to maintain a clearly identifiable housing subsidy to ensure a decent house for all households.

The first is that, although the large backlog of past housing need may have been eliminated, this does not mean that the construction of new housing units will no longer be required. For one thing, there will always be a need for new housing associated with new urban economic development: new firms, new industries, and new communities. There will also likely be a continuing need for new housing to accommodate population growth and/or migration from the rural community to the urban community. Even though there may be no housing shortage in global terms, this does not preclude housing shortages in particular localities. Moreover, even with zero population growth, as appears to be the tendency in some countries, there will still be housing needs associated with new family formation or other demographic changes, such as an aging population or increasingly identifiable groups with special needs such as the physically disabled and mentally retarded. Finally, there will always be a replacement need for new dwellings—for those units destroyed by fire, disasters, and/or town planning requirements as well as normal attrition because of depreciation and obsolescence. This is especially true of urban renewal areas in central cities where large-scale renovation is required or where there is removal of old structures and replacement by new development. In short, as long as there is a need for new construction for households which may not be able to afford the costs of that housing, it is maintained that there is justification for a separately identifiable housing subsidy policy.

Second, housing inspections are essential to ensure that subsidized housing meets minimum housing standards—a major objective of national housing policy. It would be impracticable, if not impossible, to require housing inspections as a part of general income maintenance policy. The elimination of the overall quantitative housing deficit does not ensure that all housing units in the existing stock qualitatively meet minimum housing standards.

The third reason is the powerful political appeal of the housing allowance concept. Decent living conditions are widely recognized as a "right" for everyone in an affluent, highly industrialized society. Children need a good home in order to grow up to become good adults and citizens. Adults need decent housing in order to be good parents, good workers, and good citizens. A specific subsidy for housing, therefore, has an emotional force of its own, different from and greater than a more general, abstract concept of a minimum living standard. For example, in 1981, Canadian Housing Minister Paul Cosgrave stated that housing allowances were preferable to income supplements because they dealt directly with housing affordability, they were comparatively simple to operate and apply equitably, and they allowed families to choose their own housing rather than requiring them to move into public housing projects. However, at that time, existing producer housing subsidy programs had a higher priority in the use of limited funds available.[16]

One contention has been that low-income and middle-income families are likely to be much more successful in obtaining legislation providing adequate financial assistance for decent housing or in defending existing housing financial assistance against efforts to cut it if the housing subsidy is in the form of a specific housing allowance rather than as one component in a generalized program providing a minimum annual income to all households. In this connection, the Australian Commission on Inquiry into Poverty, while recommending a guaranteed minimum income as the basic solution to the problem of poverty, argued that until that principle was accepted in practice, special assistance to households in private rental housing should be provided in the form of supplementary assistance to pensioners and an equivalent tax credit for other renters.[17]

By focusing on housing expenditures in the household budget, public policy is better able to ensure that this high priority need is reasonably well met. If minimum housing conditions are not singled out for preferential treatment, but are to be remedied only by a general income redistribution policy, then it is much less likely that the core housing problem can be solved. For example, the threshold level of money income that would be necessary to induce all Canadian households to acquire or rent adequate accommodations was believed to be far in excess of what Canadian taxpayers would tolerate as a basic level of support in a general income maintenance system; using income transfers just to bridge the gap between the poverty line and those families who fell below it would have cost about $10.3 billion in 1979.[18]

On the other hand, in a study of the simulated impact of a 50 percent negative income tax plan (Milton Friedman's proposal) on the rehabilitation of substandard housing units compared with the actual impact of the 30-year United States public housing program, Nourse found that the improved units were approximately the same—857,000 in the former and 850,000 in the latter.[19]

A fourth argument is that housing allowances for low-income households are a justifiable offset to the preferential treatment accorded by many governments to middle-class and upper-class homeowners in the form of tax deductibility privileges for mortgage interest payments and other forms of subsidy. Since the value of tax concessions in at least seven countries exceeds total housing allowance payments (see Chapter 8, Table 11), the latter policy only mitigates the basic horizontal and vertical inequity; it does not remove it.

A further reason is that the housing allowance system directly benefits the working poor who receive comparatively little assistance under the prevailing income support programs which tend to go mainly to nonworking households. Furthermore, it is contended that the shelter allowance is more effective than the guaranteed income approach in improving work incentives of low-income families.[20]

Another practical advantage is that a housing allowance system can be adjusted to the wide variability in living costs which exists between different provinces, cities, towns, and villages, and within different parts of the same city. This is necessary to ensure equity among households. It is very difficult, if not impossible, for a general income maintenance system to take appropriate account of cost differences.[21]

Finally, it is maintained by Katz and Jackson that the housing allowance concept has an advantage over other forms of housing subsidy precisely because it has many of the attributes of the wide income maintenance approach. It provides a flexible mechanism which offers scope for rationalization and coordination with other social security programs at all levels of government and among voluntary organizations.[22]

Integration or Coordination?

Governments have many options in attempting to work out an accommodation between the housing allowance system and the income security system. Two interesting cases are to be found in Canada and the United Kingdom.

Canada

In the middle of the 1970s the Canadian government appointed a high-level commission to examine the role of shelter costs in the income security system. The commission identified the following three major options for resolving the overlap and inequities in the systems catering to the two major clienteles: current welfare recipients; and the working poor.[23]

- A major extension of a housing allowance as a supplement to the welfare system. This option would direct financial assistance only to those on welfare on the assumption that such families were in greatest need. A housing allowance would be a legitimate form of income supplement since the government viewed housing as a merit good. The difficulty with this option was that it assumed that welfare eligibility criteria were appropriate for the housing authority. The fact was that many facing severe housing problems were not on welfare.

- Retargeting the housing allowance to those not receiving welfare. This option started from the assumption that it was not the responsibility of the housing authority to provide welfare. Rather housing affordability problems needed to be defined independently of welfare criteria, e.g., in terms of price, vacancy rates, and quality of the housing stock. In high-price housing markets, many households facing affordability problems had incomes above the welfare cutoff point. The problem with this option was that it failed to recognize that welfare households in high-price housing markets continued to face affordability problems.

- Housing subsidies as a complement to income security. This approach started from the assumption that the income security system should enable the typical recipient to consume adequate food, clothing, shelter, and other discretionary items. The nonhousing items could be covered by the use of standard budgets, since they could be easily transported and their prices did not vary substantially across the province. Housing was a fixed durable good, however, with prices varying greatly between markets.

In the third option, which the Task Force supported, the housing allowance should be directed to those markets where the cost of shelter, including utilities, was highest, since it was there that rent burdens were excessive. All households having affordability problems would be eligible for a housing allowance regardless of source of income. To avoid the welfare system placing an undue burden on the housing allowance system, it was necessary for the former to ensure that the basic needs of the typical recipient were covered by regular welfare payments. And to avoid creating inflationary pressures, government policy should use producer housing subsidies as well as consumer housing subsidies to bring housing supply and demand into equilibrium.

In short, the role of the housing authority should be "not the provision of welfare assistance, but the selective provision of assistance in housing markets where prices are extremely high."[24] During the ensuing years, the Canadian government has continued to debate the merits of a national housing allowance system without embarking on a new policy.[25]

The political difficulties for the Canadian federal government embarking on a national housing allowance program during the late 1970s and early 1980s have been underlined by Robert Adamson, retired Vice-President of the Canada Mortgage and Housing Corporation. First, national priorities were dominated by the issues of inflation, unemployment, and interest rates; housing was among the main victims of interest rate escalation. Second, at a time of fiscal restraint, no housing allowance program could be adopted without a "pretty big bite from the federal budget." Third, it would have required a long, tedious, and demanding federal-provincial consultation at the ministerial level that would have been very difficult considering the temper of the times. Fourth, a system of housing allowances compatible with broad social policies at the federal level would have required a far greater degree of consensus than existed.[26]

The United Kingdom

In the United Kingdom, as observed in the first section of this chapter, the role of the housing allowance in the income security system has long been a controversial issue. In March, 1981, the Department of the Environment issued a consultative document outlining a proposed reform to integrate the housing allowance system serving mainly the working poor with the income security system serving the dependent poor. The reform had several objectives:

• To be fair to recipients in similar circumstances and for those both in and out of work;
• to make the systems easily understandable;
• to minimize losses to individuals resulting therefrom; and
• to streamline and lower the costs of administration.

Under the new system all payments were calculated and administered by local authorities. Households receiving welfare payments would, if eligible, continue to receive full assistance on rents and property taxes (which in the United Kingdom are paid by the renter as well as the homeowner) without further income assessment by local authorities. The eligibility requirements for the housing allowance system would be harmonized with those of the supplementary benefit system. Households destined to receive less financial assistance as a result of the reform, e.g., certain pensioners, would receive a "topping up" payment to offset the loss. Tenants facing markedly higher rents and property taxes than on the average would receive special treatment. For example, when weekly rents exceeded $23 (£10 in 1980 prices) instead of paying 40 percent of the rent, a tenant would pay only 15 percent of the rent plus $5.80 (£2.5).[27]

Considerable difficulties have been encountered in implementing the reform. The Department of Health and Social Security encountered delays in issuing certificates to claimants for supplementary benefit. The new payment—the housing benefit supplement introduced to compensate claimants for losses that they would otherwise incur under the new plan— has been confusing. Projected economies to be achieved by administrative simplification and computerization have failed to materialize; in fact, administrative costs are higher than before. As a consequence, in early 1984, Norman Fowler, Minister of Social Services, set up a committee to review the whole system.[28]

Much valuable material and many useful suggestions were submitted to the Government's Housing Benefit Review by public and private organizations, although the terms of reference were restricted by the exclusion of tax relief on mortgage interest and general housing policy issues.[29] There was general agreement that many administrative difficulties arose from structural problems inherent in the institutional arrangements, where two agencies—the Department of Health and Social Security and local authorities—were involved in the administration, and that, accordingly, the only solution was to combine the supplementary benefit and the housing benefit.

Some Basic Elements

Foreign experience does not appear to provide clear guidelines as to how, or in what degree, housing allowance programs should be integrated or coordinated with income maintenance systems. But certain basic issues emerge that need to be and are being tackled in attempting to overcome the inequities and inefficiencies of existing disparate arrangements.

Perhaps the first issue is the development of uniform definitions of income for the various systems. Is only the income of the head of the household to be considered, or are the incomes of all members of the family—or the household—to be included? Are various forms of income transfer, such as unemployment compensation, disability pensions, or children's allowances, to be considered as income? What deductions from gross income (however defined) are to be permitted? European governments have given a great amount of attention to this problem in developing their housing allowance systems.

Second, the formulation of generally applicable eligibility requirements is a sound principle, save perhaps in special circumstances. Since income support systems tended to develop incrementally in response to specific needs, eligibility requirements often differ unnecessarily from program to program. Considerable efforts are being made to achieve greater uniformity.

Third, formulas for computing benefits for various income transfer programs should, insofar as practicable, be simple and comparable. It is highly desirable that beneficiaries understand and easily calculate their own benefit payments, and that they see that in any particular program they are not being discriminated against as compared to another program in which they are not participating. European governments have made much progress in eliminating discrepancies between various groups, e.g., as regards reasonable shelter-to-income ratios in various housing subsidy programs.

A fourth consideration is better identification of the needy categories of the population. An overall effort needs to be made to identify gaps between different kinds of income support and to ensure that the housing requirements of any particular category of the population, e.g., young single persons or immigrant workers and their families, are not ignored.

Fifth, there is the question of adequacy. Efforts to coordinate and integrate income transfer programs need to aim constantly at a payment level that will have a substantial impact in eliminating poverty, particularly for the poorest families.

Sixth, it is essential that income maintenance programs, including housing subsidy programs, be designed in such a way as to preserve and enhance work incentives. By definition a vibrant society and a viable economy are dependent on a creative and productive work environment. This is an extremely complex and delicate issue, on which most governments are working intensely.

Finally, management systems for implementing income support programs need to be consolidated, streamlined, and made more scientific. The concept of a single universal administrative structure for all income transfer programs may be of dubious value, but governments are making progress in developing more integrated and efficient administrative systems.

Summary

A satisfactory, workable integration or coordination of the housing allowance with general income maintenance policy has not yet been developed.

There appears to be a widespread view among social administrators in many highly industrialized countries that on social grounds the ideal, long-term way of eliminating the deprivations suffered by the poor, including substandard housing and excessive rent burdens, is through some kind of general income maintenance program. But this view encounters financial and philosophical objections. Fiscal administrators dispute this solution on financial grounds; such an undertaking would overload the public budget. Ideologues dispute the solution on psychological and philosophical grounds; such a solution undervalues the importance of the work ethic as a principle for organizing the social fabric of the community.

In the final analysis, perhaps the major stumbling block is adequacy. If national policy should terminate housing subsidy systems in favor of general income support, would the housing needs of the poor be better tended to—or less well tended to—than under the existing housing assistance programs? At this stage of social development, most governments seem to say that if housing subsidy programs were to be folded into a general income maintenance policy, the high priority housing needs of low-income families would not be as satisfactorily met as under existing arrangements.

But whether housing allowance programs ultimately are to be fully integrated with–or only coordinated with–income maintenance systems, there are at least seven specific issues that the two systems need to address and develop in consonance:

- More uniform income definitions;
- more uniform eligibility requirements;
- simpler and more comparable formulas for benefit payments;
- better identification of the needy categories of the population;
- greater program adequacy in coping with poverty;
- preservation and enhancement of work incentives; and
- streamlining of management systems.

NOTES

1. Central Mortgage and Housing Corporation, *Report 1 of the Task Force on Shelter and Incomes* (Ottawa: Central Mortgage and Housing Corporation, 1976), 42-43.

2. *Ibid.*, 40.

3. United Kingdom, Department of the Environment, *Assistance With Housing Costs: Consultative Document* (London: Department of the Environment, 1981), 1-2.

4. David Donnison, "A Rationalization of Housing Benefits," *Three Banks' Review* (September 1981), 4-5.

5. For a general survey of proposals *see* Robert Theobold, ed., *The Guaranteed Income: Next Step in Economic Evolution* (New York: Doubleday, 1966); Clair Wilcox, *Toward Social Welfare* (Homewood, IL: Richard D. Irvin, 1969), 248-69; John B. Williamson and Jerry F. Boren, *Strategies Against Poverty in America* (New York: Schenkman, 1975); and James R. Storey et al., *The Better Jobs and Income Plan* (Washington, D.C.: Urban Institute, 1978).

6. *See* United Nations Economic Commission for Europe, Committee on Housing, Building and Planning, *Financing of Housing* (Geneva: United Nations Economic Commission for Europe, 1973), 20.

7. Janet McClain (ed.), *Are Housing Allowances the Answer?* (Ottawa: Canadian Council on Social Development, 1979), 3.

8. Peter H. Rossi, Andy B. Anderson, and James D. Wright, *Housing Consumption Effects of Guaranteed Annual Income Experiments* (Ottawa: Canada Mortgage and Housing Corporation, 1982), 104.

9. International Social Security Association, *Study of Some Economic Aspects of Family Allowances* (Geneva: International Social Security Association, 1970); International Labour Office, *Possibility of Adopting an International Instrument Dealing With Family Benefits* (Geneva: International Labour Office, 1967).

10. Cited in K. F. Watson, F. Ermuth, and W. Hamilton, *A Comparative Analysis of Housing Allowance Programs* (Ottawa: Central Mortgage and Housing Corporation, 1978), E-23.

11. Janet McClain, ed., *op. cit.,* 5. *See also* Canadian Council on Social Development, *Income Supplements for the Working Poor* (Ottawa: Canadian Council on Social Development, 1974).

12. Cited by Marion Steele in her unpublished study of housing allowances for the Ontario Economic Council in 1982, Chaps. 8, 21. Author's address: Department of Economics, University of Guelph, Guelph, Ontario, N1G 2W1, Canada.

13. Milton Friedman, *Capitalism and Freedom* (Chicago: University of Chicago Press, 1962), 190-95.

14. *See* Irene Lurie (ed.) *Integrating Income Maintenance Programs* (New York: Academic Press, 1975); United States General Accounting Office, *U.S. Income Security System Needs Leadership, Policy and Effective Management* (Washington, D.C.: U.S. General Accounting Office, 1980); United States General Accounting Office, *Millions Can Be Saved by Improving the Productivity of State and Local Governments Administering Federal Income Maintenance Assistance Programs* (Washington, D.C.: U.S. General Accounting Office, 1981).

15. H. W. Richardson, *Regional and Urban Economics* (London: Penguin, 1978), 352-55; D. C. Stafford, *The Economics of Housing Policy* (London: Croom Helm, 1978), 68-69; Michael John Oxley, "Housing Policy in Western Europe: An Economic Analysis of the Aims and Instruments of Housing Policy in the United Kingdom, West Germany, France, the Netherlands, Denmark and Ireland" (Ph.D. diss., Leicester Polytechnic University, 1983), 306-12.

16. "Cosgrove Hints at Housing Allowance Program," *Housing Ontario* (March-April 1981), 27.

17. Australia, Commission of Inquiry Into Poverty, *First Main Report* (Canberra: AGPS, 1975), 160.

18. Canada, Interdepartmental Task Force, *Some Considerations for Interdepartmental Task Force on Shelter Allowances* (Ottawa: n.p., 1979), Sec. 3.1.2.

19. Hugh O. Nourse, *Impact of a Negative Income Tax on the Number of Substandard Housing Units* (Madison, WI: Institute for Research on Poverty, University of Wisconsin, 1969), 1.

20. Derek Hum & Associates, Ltd., *Shelter Allowances and Work Incentives: An Exploratory Assessment* (Ottawa: Canada Mortgage and Housing Corporation, 1981).

21. Canada, Interdepartmental Task Force, *op. cit.,* Sec. 3.2.

22. Arnold J. Katz and Wayne S. B. Jackson, "The Australian Housing Allowance Voucher Experiment: A Venture in Social Policy Development," *Social and Economic Administration,* Vol. 12 (Winter 1978), 200.

23. Canada, Task Force on Shelter and Incomes, *Report 1* (Ottawa: Central Mortgage and Housing Corporation, 1976), 43-47.

24. *Ibid.,* 47.

25. Patricia Streich, "The Evolution of Housing Allowances in Canada" in, *And Where Do We Go From Here?,* ed., Janet McClain, (Ottawa: Canadian Council on Social Development, 1983), 47-56.

26. Robert Adamson, "Putting the Symposium in Perspective," in *ibid.,* 125-26.

27. United Kingdom, Department of the Environment, *op. cit.* 6.

28. "Housing Benefit Falling Down," *The Economist* (London, February 11, 1984), 54-55.

29. Peter Kemp and Nick Raynsford, *Housing Benefit: The Evidence. A Collection of Submissions to the Housing Benefit Review* (London: Housing Centre Bookshop, 1984). *See also* Malcolm Boorer, "More Thoughts on the Future of Housing Benefit," *Housing Review* (November-December 1984), 231-32.

12

Conclusions

Strategies of Foreign Housing Allowance Systems

Housing allowance systems originated rather piecemeal and have been revised and expanded in response to specific needs that surfaced in national housing policy. Eight rather distinct housing allowance models can be distinguished.

The first was the large family hardship model. A great moral concern of the day was the welfare of children born in urban slums: How could they grow up to be responsible citizens, hard workers, and good parents if they were not raised in a decent home? The housing allowance provided a simple tool to improve the quality of life for the many children in large families.

The second model focused on elderly hardship. Again the housing allowance was a convenient means to target supplementary assistance to the elderly poor who—on small fixed pensions or little income—were suffering from creeping inflation.

The rent harmonization model was a third significant variant. Governments were anxious to relax wartime rent controls and restore efficient housing markets. To minimize hardship for households living on fixed incomes and to make a politically unpopular policy more palatable, in some countries housing allowance systems became a strategic factor in preventing financial suffering that might result from step-by-step removal of rent controls.

In the emerging Age of Affluence, governments became increasingly sensitive to the housing affordability problem. As the huge backlog of housing demand inherited from the Great Depression and World War II was gradually eliminated, an increasingly important objective of national housing subsidy policy was to relieve the excessive shelter-to-income burden on low-income families. This was the excessive shelter-to-income model.

Most governments have also been confronted with a growing gap between the rents of new housing built at high cost levels and the rents of existing housing built at much lower cost levels. To facilitate the unloading of new, modern apartments on a clientele who could not otherwise afford them, the tandem–new construction model became an effective tool in supplementing producer housing subsidy programs.

Social stability ranks high in the traditional European value system. Eviction of a household because of inability to pay rent is considered a serious threat to social stability, the sixth model. It is not surprising, therefore, that the animus of housing allowance systems frequently was to strengthen the ability of financially weak households to hang on to the housing they had.

A seventh labor mobility model was a government response to a housing market long under the heavy hand of rent controls. Greater labor mobility was urgently needed to support high national economic growth rates. Housing allowances became an admirable means of inducing older couples to give up large apartments as children left home and of offering an incentive to workers to rent new, high-cost accommodations in expanding urban areas.

A final interesting concept was developed in the family crisis model. The housing allowance could be an effective short-term, financial support to low-income families confronted with temporary household crises, such as the loss of job or ill health of the breadwinner(s).

Designing Housing Allowance Formulas

Probably the central problem in housing subsidy policy is the gap between what workers can afford to pay for shelter and what they must pay for decent accommodations in the housing market. This is the affordability problem. In attempting to bridge this gap, there are two general ways of constructing the housing allowance formula: the percentage of gap method; and the percentage of rent method.

The percentage of gap method determines the monthly cost of decent housing and subtracts from that amount what the family can afford to pay, expressed as a percentage of its income; the housing allowance then covers all or a part of the difference. The percentage of rent method brings the cost of housing down to what the family can afford by paying the family a certain percent of the monthly cost of decent housing. Practically all governments have adopted the former method.

In developing housing allowance formulas, four major elements are involved: a reasonable shelter-to-income ratio; a reasonable household income ceiling; a reasonable household rent ceiling; and a reasonable percentage coverage of the unaffordable gap.

Shelter-to-Income Ratio

In establishing a reasonable shelter-to-income ratio that households should spend on housing, two major factors have influenced government policy: the level of income and the number of children.

At very low levels of income, some governments, e.g., Austria, France (in its early system), and the United Kingdom, place the percentage of income that should be spent on housing at zero, the belief being that all income is needed for the basic necessities of life exclusive of shelter. Other countries have taken the position that every family should—as a matter of principle—pay a minimum rent, ranging from 7 to 11 percent of income. As household income rises, the affordable ratio is generally increased, the maximum being in the range of 15 to 25 percent of adjusted or taxable income.

As regards the second element, the number of children, in most systems the maximum percentage of income that should be paid for shelter declines as the number of children increases.

Household Income Ceiling

Practically all governments established income ceilings for housing allowance participants. It is certainly unreasonable to expect the taxpayer to continue subsidizing a family if its income rises to the point that it can afford to pay the rent.

A few governments established a formal income ceiling comparable to United States practice; for example, the Netherlands has a cutoff point at the 75th percentile of income. Other countries established ceilings indirectly through the application of other limits to family size, size of dwelling, and rent ceilings.

Methods of computing income vary considerably. The most widely used definition of income for housing allowance purposes is taxable income. Some governments, however, start with gross household income and allow certain deductions.

Most governments have some arrangement—delayed though it may be—for income ceilings to be periodically adjusted upwards to allow for inflation.

Rent Ceiling

The third major element in designing a housing allowance is the economic cost of minimum standard housing; public policy cannot be expected to make an unlimited commitment to providing housing financial assistance. The most widely used guide in establishing rent ceilings appears to have been, implicitly if not explicitly, the average rent of minimum standard housing in the housing market area. In applying this general principle, governments introduced additional criteria, such as the number and sex of family members, size of community, and age of dwelling. It is customary to publicize rent ceiling tariffs.

Unaffordable Gap to Be Covered by Subsidy

Having determined the size of the gap between the market rent for decent housing and what families can afford to pay, the final issue is: What part of the gap should be covered by government subsidy?

A strong moral case can be made that 100 percent of the gap should be covered by the housing allowance; otherwise the cost of shelter exceeds what the family can afford to pay with the resulting sacrifice of other vital elements in its level of living. A number of systems pay 100 percent of the gap.

On the other hand, a majority of systems cover only part of the gap, the percentage ranging from 50 to 90 percent. The reasons for this policy are twofold. Covering 100 percent of the gap involves too heavy a tax burden. Furthermore, it may encourage families to overconsume housing services, that is, to acquire above minimum standard housing at higher rents than are appropriate.

In a striking innovation, Sweden pays the highest percentage of the gap for more expensive dwelling units and the lowest percentage for less expensive dwellings (always within overall rent ceilings). The social purpose is to increase the quality of housing in regard to living space, particularly for large families.

Qualifying Conditions

Housing allowance systems have established a variety of qualifying conditions. The foremost requirement has been that the physical structure of the dwelling should meet minimum housing standards. Some countries, such as France, set up detailed rules, while other countries, such as the Federal Republic of Germany, have only general prescriptions.

Two other important related conditions helped to reinforce the objective that participants live in minimum standard housing. First, some countries limited the housing allowance to families living in housing financed or owned by public authorities. Second, many systems have declared families living in old housing, defined, for example, as pre-World War II housing or housing built before a more recent cutoff date, such as 1960, as ineligible. Such restrictions automatically exclude much of the substandard housing stock from housing allowance systems.

It should be observed, however, that some countries, such as the Federal Republic of Germany, Finland, the Netherlands, Sweden, and the United Kingdom, do not make minimum standards a condition for receiving the allowance. This may be explained by the fact that housing inspections are costly, that tying the housing allowance to minimum standard requirements may discourage many households from applying, and that in some countries the housing stock is of such good quality that it needs little monitoring.

In the early days of housing allowance systems, eligibility was restricted to certain types of households that were particularly subject to hardship, for example, large families and the elderly. However, eligibility requirements have been gradually expanded so that now most programs include nearly all low-income households.

Tenure is another qualifying condition. Countries are about evenly divided among those which include and those which exclude homeowners in their housing allowance programs. In practice, however, even in those systems which include them, homeowners constitute a relatively small percentage of participants, since comparatively few fall into the low-income category.

Administrative Arrangements

Foreign governments have encountered enrollment problems. The enrollment level, ranging from 50 to 90 percent, has, however, been higher than the 33 to 50 percent rate in the United States Experimental Housing Allowance Program.

The reasons for the disappointing enrollment are many. Pride often prevents a family from accepting what may be regarded as charity. Furthermore, passing the means test to qualify may be seen as demeaning. In some cases, bureaucratic procedures seemed formidable; in other cases tenants feared landlord disapproval; while in still other instances, the allowance has been so small it was not believed worth bothering about. Oftentimes families preferred to live in substandard housing in familiar, friendly surroundings rather than move to a new community in order to obtain a housing allowance. A major factor has been that the poorest families have frequently been the least educated and least capable of reading brochures and filling out application forms.

Several measures have been taken to increase enrollment. Governments have embarked on national publicity campaigns to educate potential participants, but with dubious results. The United Kingdom used trained canvassers to generate applications, with modest results. Sweden used the income tax system to stimulate enrollment. Application forms and enrollment instructions have been sent to households that were potentially eligible according to a computer screening of income tax returns.

Recertification of continued eligibility takes place generally on an annual basis. Sweden appears to have developed an effective monitoring system using its income tax machinery.

Normally housing allowances are paid directly to the occupant, although in a number of systems they may be paid to the owner instead. The usual practice is for payment to be made monthly in arrears, although in some systems, it is paid on a weekly or quarterly basis. In the Federal Republic of Germany, it is paid in advance.

Various support services have been provided by governments, such as counseling in the United Kingdom or removal grants in the Netherlands. But such services do not appear to have been extensively developed.

In those countries having two or more housing allowance systems, efforts are increasingly being made to coordinate and integrate these plans so as to remove inequities among recipients. Administrative costs vary widely, ranging from 2.5 percent in Finland and 3 percent in Denmark to around 15 and 17 percent of program costs, respectively, in France and the United Kingdom.

Impact of Housing Allowances

The two principal objectives of housing subsidy policy are to improve physical living conditions and to reduce excessive rent burdens on low-income families. As regards the first, the impact appears to have been considerable, although on the whole indirect. At the time they initially receive assistance, the great majority of housing allowance recipients already live in minimum standard housing. In the short run, the allowance has been a positive factor in promoting housing rehabilitation. In the long run, the increased demand for minimum standard housing has undoubtedly stimulated additional new construction.

As regards the second objective, the housing allowance has been highly successful in making housing costs a more reasonable charge on the family budget. Moreover, it has been effective in targeting assistance to special hardship households, such as large families and the elderly. Housing allowances also achieved some success in facilitating a relaxation of rent regulations and in promoting two other major national objectives—greater labor mobility and the maintenance of social stability.

Consumer Subsidy Approach Versus Producer Subsidy Approach

One of the foremost European housing subsidy issues concerns the relative roles which the consumer and the producer housing subsidy approaches should play in national policy. In an evaluation of European experience with the two systems, according to the five following criteria the consumer subsidy system emerges superior: 1) reducing excessive rent burdens; 2) minimizing housing costs; 3) ensuring equity; 4) promoting freedom of choice of abode; and 5) promoting effective use of the existing housing stock. On the other hand, the producer subsidy approach has the advantage according to the following measures: 1) improving housing conditions; 2) protecting the value of the housing subsidy; and 3) administrative simplicity.

In broad philosophical terms, the consumer subsidy system appears to enjoy greatest favor; in fact two governments—France and Sweden—have shown preference for this system in national policy. The reality is, however, that in terms of percentage of total annual national housing subsidies, the housing allowance remains the smaller share in all countries.

The explanation for this contradiction is not entirely clear. The reason appears to be the persistence of serious housing supply problems. Notwithstanding the elimination of the overall backlog of housing demand inherited from the Great Depression and World War II, and notwithstanding periodic feelings and statements that housing supply has caught up with housing demand, and that accordingly national attention can shift from the quantitative to the qualitative aspects of the housing stock, producer housing subsidies still exceed consumer housing subsidies. Unanticipated new housing demands, attributable to such factors as higher rates of household formation, higher housing aspirations accompanying rising affluence, and greater dependence on a foreign labor supply, have resulted in continuing visible housing shortages. Moreover, there seems to be a lack of confidence that even with a housing allowance system, the private housing market will, in fact, meet the remaining unfilled housing needs of certain low-income groups, such as the elderly, large families, and immigrant workers.

One anomaly in many foreign housing subsidy systems—as in the United States—is the large subsidy extended to homeowners through tax deductibility of mortgage interest payments. Australia and Canada do not have such a subsidy.

European housing subsidy policy involves a mix which is concerned perhaps foremost with the affordability problem, but which at the same time uses producer subsidies to focus improvement on high priority sectors of housing need such as urban renewal in inner cities.

Housing Allowance Versus General Income Maintenance Policy

There is a widespread view that the housing allowance really is an income transfer policy and not a housing policy; therefore, it should be integrated with general income maintenance programs (which include the welfare system and the social insurance system for the unemployed, sick, retired, and single parent caring for children). This view maintains further that there is no longer a housing availability problem; rather it is a question of affordability. The shortage is of income, not of housing space. Some governments have, in fact, not made minimum housing standards a condition of payment. In short, merging the housing allowance system with a general income support program, e.g., through a minimum or guaranteed annual income, would not only make for administrative simplification but would also give the worker complete freedom to spend income in accordance with his preferences and thus maximize consumer satisfaction. This, it is contended, is the most effective way of dealing with poverty.

However, most foreign governments seem little disposed to fold housing allowance systems into general income maintenance systems. First, some form of housing inspection or monitoring accompanying most housing allowance systems is generally essential to ensure that subsidized housing programs meet minimum housing standards—a major objective of national housing policy. It would be impracticable, if not impossible, to require housing inspections or monitoring as a part of general income maintenance policy.

Second, the housing allowance has powerful political appeal in defending existing financial assistance against efforts to cut or abolish it. Third, the housing allowance provides needed assistance for the working poor, whom general income maintenance plans are not normally intended to cover. Fourth, although there may no longer be a serious global housing deficiency, local shortages do persist. The general view seems to be that there will always be a need for housing programs for households that are not able to afford the costs of that housing. Thus, a satisfactory synthesis of the housing allowance with the general income maintenance system has yet to be worked out.

Whether housing allowance programs ultimately are to be fully integrated with–or only coordinated with–income maintenance systems, there are at least seven specific issues that the two systems need to address and develop in consonance:

- More uniform income definitions;
- more uniform eligibility requirements;
- simpler and more comparable formulas for benefit payments;
- better identification of the needy categories of the population;
- greater program adequacy in coping with poverty;
- preservation and enhancement of work incentives; and
- streamlining of management systems.

Bibliography on Foreign Experience

Andrzejewski, A. and Lujanen, Martti. *Major Trends in Housing Policy in ECE Countries*. New York: United Nations, 1980.

Angelini, Terenzio and Gurtner, Peter. *Marche et Politique du Logement en Suisse*. Berne: Office Federal du Logement, 1978.

Association of Municipalities of Ontario. *Shelter Allowances*. Toronto: The Association of Municipalities of Ontario, 1980.

Australia, Commission of Inquiry into Poverty. *First Main Report*. Canberra: Australian Government Publishing Service, 1975.

_____, Commonwealth Housing Commission. *Final Report*. Sydney: Ministry of Post-War Reconstruction, 1944.

_____, Department of Environment, Housing and Community Development. *Housing Allowance Experiment: Final Design*. 2 vols. Canberra: Department of Environment, Housing and Community Development, 1978.

_____, Department of Housing and Construction. *Housing Assistance Act, 1981* (Annual Report for the Year, 1981-82). Canberra: Department of Housing and Construction, 1983.

_____, Department of Works and Housing. *Homes for Australia*. Canberra: Department of Works and Housing, 1949.

Austria, Ministry of Construction and Technology. *Current Trends and Policies in the Field of Housing, Building and Planning*. Vienna: Ministry of Construction and Technology, 1980.

Barre, Raymond et al. *Report of a Commission to Study Reform of the Financing of Housing*. Germantown, MD: HUD USER, 1975. (Translation of *Rapport de la Commission d'Etude d'une Reforme du Financement du Logement*. Paris: Ministry for City Planning and Housing, 1975.)

Belgium, Housing and Family Welfare Administration. *Social Housing Policy in Belgium.* Germantown, MD: HUD USER, 1969. Translation.

Boorer, Malcolm. "More Thoughts on the Future of Housing Benefit." *Housing Review* (November-December 1984), 231-32.

British Columbia, Ministry of Municipal Affairs and Housing. *Profile of the SAFER Beneficiaries.* Vancouver, Canada: Ministry of Municipal Affairs and Housing, 1978.

Canada, Mortgage and Housing Corporation. *Provincial Shelter Allowance Programs.* Ottawa: Mortgage and Housing Corporation, 1981.

_____, Federal Task Force on Housing and Urban Development. *Report.* Ottawa: Queen's Printer, 1969.

_____, Task Force on Shelter and Incomes. *Report 1 of the Task Force on Shelter and Incomes.* Ottawa: Central Mortgage and Housing Corporation, 1976.

Canadian Council on Social Development. *Income Supplements for the Working Poor.* Ottawa: Canadian Council on Social Development, 1974.

Clayton Research Associates. *The Impacts of Shelter Allowances.* Ottawa: Canada Mortgage and Housing Corporation, 1981.

Cocks, Freda. "Housing Allowances for Private Tenants—Birmingham's Experiences." *Housing Review* (January-February 1972), 25.

"Cosgrove Hints at Housing Allowance Program." *Housing Ontario* (March-April 1981), 26-27.

Cullingworth, J. Barry. *Essays on Housing Policy.* London: Allen and Unwin, 1979.

_____. *Housing Allowances: The British Experience.* Toronto: Centre for Community Studies, University of Toronto, 1977.

Denmark, Ministry of Housing. "Financing of Housing Subsidies in Denmark." Paper prepared for United Nations Economic Commission for Europe, Committee on Housing, Building and Planning, Seminar on Financing of Housing. Copenhagen: Ministry of Housing, 1985.

_____. *Human Settlements Situation and Related Trends and Policies.* Copenhagen: Ministry of Housing, 1982.

Dennis, Michael and Fish, Susan. *Programs in Search of a Policy: Low Income Housing in Canada.* Toronto: Hakkert, 1972.

Denton, Frank T.; Robb, A. Leslie; and Spencer, Byron G. *The Economics of Shelter Allowances.* Ottawa: Canada Mortgage and Housing Corporation, 1982.

Dick, Eugen. "Distribution of Housing Costs Between the Public Sector and Individuals." Paper prepared for the United Nations

Economic Commission for Europe, Committee on Housing, Building and Planning, Seminar on Housing Policy. Turku, Finland, 1977 (Bonn: Ministry for Regional Planning, Building and Urban Development, 1977).

————. "Wohngeld." Paper prepared for the United Nations Economic Commission for Europe, Committee on Housing, Building, and Planning, Seminar on Financing of Housing. Copenhagen, Denmark, 1985. Bonn: Ministry for Regional Planning, Building and Urban Development, 1985.

Donnison, David. "A Rationalization of Housing Benefits." *Three Banks' Review* (September 1981), 1-14.

————. *The Government of Housing.* London: Penguin, 1967.

Eines, Birger. *The Rent Grant System (Rent Allocation)—A Selective Subsidy.* Oslo, 1977. Privately mimeographed.

Field, Tim. "Pensioners Who Rent: Problems and Alternatives." *Social Security Journal* (Canberra, June 1983), 25-28.

Finland, Ministry of the Interior and National Housing Board. *Human Settlements Situation and Related Trends and Policies.* Helsinki: Ministry of Interior and National Housing Board, 1982.

Forma Consulting. *A Brief Review of the International Experience With Housing Allowances.* Ottawa: Central Mortgage and Housing Corporation, 1978.

France, Ministry for City Planning and Housing. *L'Aide Personnalisee au Logement* (Paris: Ministry for City Planning and Housing, 1978); *Human Habitation in France: Situation, Tendencies and Policies.* (Paris: Ministry for City Planning and Housing, 1984).

————. *Repartition des Aides de l'Etat au Logement Par Nature de Financement.* Paris: Ministry for City Planning and Housing, 1984.

————. *Report of the Working Group on the Reform of Personal Housing Assistance.* Germantown, MD: HUD USER, 1982. Translation of *Rapport du Groupe de Travail sur des Aides Personnelles au Logement.* Jacques Badet, Chairman (Paris: Ministry for City Planning and Housing, 1982).

————. Ministere de l'Equipement. *La Reforme du Logement* (December-January 1977).

Frommes, Robert. *Problems Raised by the Individual Subsidization of Accommodation.* The Hague: International Federation of Housing and Planning, 1970.

German Marshall Fund of the United States. *U.S./British/German Discussion of Housing Policy.* Washington, D.C.: German Marshall Fund of the United States, 1979.

Germany, Federal Republic of, Ministry for Regional Planning, Building and Urban Development. *Housing Allowance and Rent: 1983 Report.* Germantown, MD: HUD USER, 1983. Translation.

————. *Monograph on the Human Settlements Situation and Related Trends and Policies.* Bonn: Ministry for Regional Planning, Building and Urban Development, 1982.

————. *Rent Allowance and Rent Report.* Germantown, MD: HUD USER, 1977. Translation.

————. *Rent Allowance '78.* Germantown, MD: HUD USER 1977.

Golob, Laura. "Rent Supplement—Everyone Likes It—Including the Private Landlords." *Housing Ontario* (June 1975), 2-4.

Howenstine, E. Jay. *Attacking Housing Costs.* New Brunswick, NJ: Center for Urban Policy Research, Rutgers University, 1983.

————. "European Experience with Rent Controls." *Monthly Labor Review* (June 1977), 21-28.

————. *Foreign Housing Subsidy Systems.* Springfield, VA: National Technical Information Service, U.S. Department of Commerce, 1973.

————. "Private Rental Housing Abroad: Dwindling Supply Stirs Concern," *Monthly Labor Review* (September 1981), 38-42.

————. "Rental Housing in Industrialized Countries: Issues and Policies," in *Rental Housing: Is There a Crisis?* edited by John C. Weicher, Kevin E. Villani, and Elizabeth A. Roistacher. Washington, D.C.: Urban Institute, 1981, 103-107.

————. "The Changing Roles of Housing Production Subsidies and Consumer Housing Subsidies in European National Housing Policy." *Land Economics* (February 1975), 86-94.

Hum, Derek & Associates, Ltd. *Shelter Allowances and Work Incentives: An Exploratory Assessment.* Ottawa: Canada Mortgage and Housing Corporation, 1981.

International Labour Office. *International Labour Conventions and Recommendations, 1919–1981.* Geneva: International Labour Office, 1982.

————. *International Survey of Social Security: Comparative Analysis and Summary of National Laws.* Geneva: International Labour Office, 1950.

————. *Introduction to Social Security.* Geneva: International Labour Office, 1984.

————, Committee of Social Security Experts. *Possibility of Adopting an International Instrument Dealing with Family Benefits.* Geneva: International Labour Office, 1967.

International Social Security Association. *Study of Some Economic Aspects of Family Allowances.* Geneva: International Social Security Association, 1970.

Ireland, Department of the Environment. *A Home of Your Own.* Dublin: Department of the Environment, 1978.

_____. *Current Trends and Policies in the Field of Housing, Building and Planning.* Dublin: Department of the Environment, 1980.

_____, National Economic and Social Council. *Report on Housing Subsidies.* Dublin: National Economic and Social Council, 1977.

_____, National Institute for Physical Planning and Construction Research. *Public Subventions to Housing in Ireland.* Dublin: National Institute for Physical Planning and Construction Research, 1978.

Johnson, Jeremy J. *Housing Vouchers: A Selective Bibliography.* Adelaide, Australia: South Australian Housing Trust, 1977.

Katz, Arnold J. and Jackson, Wayne S. B. "The Australian Housing Allowance Voucher Experiment: A Venture in Social Policy Development." *Social and Economic Administration* (Winter 1978), 197-208.

Kemp, Peter and Raynsford, Nick. *Housing Benefit: The Evidence. A Collection of Submissions to the Housing Benefit Review.* London: Housing Centre Bookshop, 1984.

Legg, Charles and Brion, Marion. *The Administration of the Rent Rebate and Rent Allowance Schemes.* London: Department of the Environment, 1976.

Lithwick, I. "The Derivation of Costs to Government for Providing Low-Income Housing Under Alternative Programs and Assumptions." In *Appendices to Report 1, Task Force on Shelter and Incomes,* App. H, 55-73. Ottawa: Central Mortgage and Housing Corporation, 1976.

Lundquist, Lennart J. *Housing Tenures in Sweden.* Stockholm: National Swedish Institute for Building Research, 1981.

McClain, Janet, ed. *Are Housing Allowances the Answer?* Ottawa: Canadian Council on Social Development, 1979.

_____. *And Where Do We Go From Here?* Ottawa: Canadian Council on Social Development, 1983.

MacMillian, James A. and Nickel, Edith. "An Economic Appraisal of Urban Housing Assistance: Rental Supplements Versus Public Housing." *Canadian Public Administration* (Fall 1974), 443-60.

Manitoba, Manitoba Housing and Renewal Corporation. *SAFER: Shelter Allowances for Elderly Renters.* Winnipeg, Canada: Manitoba Housing and Renewal Corporation, 1981.

Mayo, Stephen K. and Barnbrock, Jorn. *Rental Housing Subsidy Programs in Germany and the U.S.: A Comparative Program Evaluation.* Bonn: Bundesministerium fur Bauwesen, Raumordnung und Stadtebau, 1980.

Netherlands, the. Ministry of Housing and Physical Planning. *Current Trends and Policies in the Fields of Housing, Building and Planning.* The Hague: Ministry of Housing and Physical Planning, 1980.

————, Ministry of Housing, Physical Planning and Environment. *Some Data on House-Building in the Netherlands.* The Hague: Ministry of Housing and Physical Planning, 1983.

Nevitt, A. A. *Housing, Taxation and Subsidies.* London: Nelson, 1966.

New Brunswick. *RATE: Rental Assistance to the Elderly.* New Brunswick, Canada, 1978.

New Zealand, National Housing Commission. *Housing New Zealand.* Wellington: National Housing Commission, 1978.

Norway, Ministry of Local Government and Labour. *Current Trends and Policies in the Field of Human Settlements.* Oslo: Ministry of Local Government and Labour, 1980.

Oxley, Michael John. "Housing Policy in Western Europe: An Economic Analysis of the Aims and Instruments of Housing Policy in the United Kingdom, West Germany, France, the Netherlands, Denmark and Ireland." Ph.D. dissertation, Leicester University, United Kingdom, 1983.

Pfeiffer, U. and Stahl, K. *Housing Finance Policies in Germany.* Bonn: Ministry for Regional Planning, Building and Urban Development, 1975.

Priemus, Hugo. *Housing Allowances in the Netherlands.* Delft: Delft University Press, 1984.

————, ed. *Who Will Pay the Housing Bill in the Eighties?* Delft: Delft University Press, 1983.

Richardson, H. W. *Regional and Urban Economics.* London: Penguin, 1978.

Ricketts, Martin. "The Economics of the Rent Allowance." *Scottish Journal of Political Economy* (November 1976), 235-60.

Rose, Albert. *Canadian Housing Policies: 1935–1980.* Toronto: Buttersworth, 1980.

Rossi, Peter H.; Anderson, Andy B.; and Wright, James D. *Housing Consumption Effects of Guaranteed Annual Income Experiments.* Ottawa: Canada Mortgage and Housing Corporation, 1982.

Schneider, Oscar. "Leistungsfahiges Wohngeldsystem Unverzichtbar Anderungen Wohnungs und Sozialpolitisch Vertretbar." *Gemeinnutziges Wohnungswesen,* Vol. 2 (1983), 62-64.

Schwerz, Gunter. *Systems and Significance of Individual Subsidization of Accommodation Costs in European Countries.* Bonn: Domus-Verlag, 1966.

Smart, S. E., "The Take-up and Renewal of Rent Rebates by GLC Tenants." *Housing Monthly* (July 1975), 26.

South Australian Housing Trust. *The Rent Relief Scheme in South Australia: The First Twelve Months.* Adelaide, Australia: South Australian Housing Trust, 1984.

Stafford, D.C. *The Economics of Housing Policy.* London: Croom Helm, 1978.

Steele, Marion. "Housing Allowances." Unpublished Study for Ontario Economic Council, 1982. Author's address: Department of Economics, University of Guelph, Guelph, Ontario, Canada.

————. "The Low Consumption Response of Canadian Housing Allowance Recipients," in *And Where Do We Go From Here?*, edited by Janet McClain. Ottawa: Canadian Council on Social Development, 1983.

Streich, Patricia. "The Evolution of Housing Allowances in Canada," in *And Where Do We Go From Here?*, edited by Janet McClain. Ottawa: Canadian Council on Social Development, 1983.

Sweden, Housing Subsidy Committee. *Housing Subsidies.* Germantown, MD: HUD USER, 1982. Translation of *Bostads Bidragen.*

————. Ministry of Housing and Physical Planning. *Human Settlements in Sweden: Current Situation and Related Trends and Policies.* Stockholm: Ministry of Housing and Physical Planning, 1983.

————, National Housing Board. *Housing Allowance 1984.* Stockholm: National Housing Board, 1984.

Tanner, Keijo. *The Finnish Housing Allowance System for Families and Single Persons as Applied in 1983.* Helsinki: National Housing Board, 1983. Report available from HUD USER (Germantown, MD, 1983).

Trutko, John; Hetzel, Otto J.; and Yates, A. David. *A Comparison of the Experimental Housing Allowance Program and Great Britain's Rent Allowance Program.* Washington, D.C.: Urban Institute, 1978.

Tucker, S. N. "An Analysis of Housing Subsidy Schemes in Australia." *Urban Studies* (November 1983), 439-53.

Union Internationale des Organismes Familiaux. *Compte-Rendu, 8th Session Pleniere.* Brussels: Union Internationale des Organismes Familiaux, 1962.

————. *Cout du Logement et Integration du Loyer dans le Budget.* Brussels: Union Internationale des Organismes Familiaux, 1962.

————. *Etudes sur le Logement Familial.* Brussels: Union Internationale des Organismes Familiaux, 1955.

————. *La Mutation des Occupants de Logements dans les Quartiers d'Habitations Sociales.* Brussels: Union Internationale des Organismes Familiaux, 1962.

————. *Minimum Habitable Surfaces: Increase in Size and Cost of Dwelling in Relation to the Size of Family.* Brussels: Union Internationale des Organismes Familiaux, 1957.

United Kingdom, Department of the Environment. *Assistance with Housing Costs: Consultative Document.* London: Department of the Environment, 1981.

————. *Housing Policy: A Consultative Document.* London: Her Majesty's Stationary Office, 1977.

————. *Housing Policy: Technical Volume.* London: Her Majesty's Stationary Office, 1977.

————. *United Kingdom Monograph on the Human Settlements Situation and Related Trends and Policies.* London: Department of the Environment, 1982.

United Nations. *Compendium of Housing Statistics, 1972-74.* New York: United Nations, 1976.

————, Economic Commission for Europe. *Financing of Housing in Europe.* Geneva: United Nations, 1958.

————. *Financing of Housing.* Geneva: United Nations, Economic Commission for Europe, 1973.

————. *Housing Situation in the ECE Countries Around 1970.* New York: United Nations, 1978.

Victoria, Ministry of Housing. *Rental Subsidy Scheme for Families in Crisis.* Melbourne: Ministry of Housing, 1981.

Walker, Robert L. *Canvassing Rent Allowances in Bristol and Westminster.* London: Housing Development Directorate, Department of Environment, 1978.

Watson, K. F.; Ermuth, F.; and Hamilton, W. *A Comparative Analysis of Housing Allowance Programs.* Ottawa: Central Mortgage and Housing Corporation, 1978.

Wicks, Malcolm. "Helping the Rent Payer." *Housing Review* (September-October 1974), 128-29.

Wiewel, W. *Housing Allowances and the Dutch Rent Subsidy Program.* Santa Monica, CA: Rand Corporation, 1979.

Wynen, Lucien. *Le Financement du Logement Social.* Brussels: Union Internationale des Organismes Familiaux, 1962.

Zeyl, N. "Systems of Individual Subsidies," in *Financing of Housing,* 151-84. Geneva: United Nations Economic Commission for Europe, Committee on Housing, Building and Planning, 1973.

Index